Our Debt to Greece and Rome

EDITORS

George Depue Hadzsits, Ph.D.

University of Pennsylvania

David Moore Robinson, Ph.D., LL.D.

The Johns Hopkins University

ANCIENT EDUCATION AND ITS MEANING TO US

BY

J. F. DOBSON, M.A.

Trinity College, Cambridge

PROFESSOR OF GREEK

in the University of Bristol

LONGMANS, GREEN AND CO.

55 FIFTH AVENUE

NEW YORK

1932

DOBSON

ANCIENT EDUCATION

FIRST EDITION

PRINTED IN THE UNITED STATES OF AMERICA

CONTENTS

ANCIENT EDUCATION

ANCIENT EDUCATION

INTRODUCTION

WHAT is the true object of education? Should the educator aim at training the largest possible number of individuals to be of the greatest possible service to the State, up to the limit of the capability of each, or should he rather try to give each one an opportunity to develop fully the best qualities which he possesses, regardless of whether this method of training may or may not seem to be of immediate practical use either to the person or to the community? The question, in most ages and most countries, does not admit of a simple answer. It came nearest to being answered in Sparta, which of all nations known to history paid least attention to the individual as such, and in Republican Rome, which, though not so rigid as Sparta, regarded education as concerned mainly with the production of useful citizens.

In Rome, at least before the great development which followed on the introduction of Greek ideas, and in Sparta throughout her history, this social side of education was predominant.

In other Greek states there was at all times more of individualism. The Ionians of Asia Minor represent the extreme of the opposite attitude, and even democratic Athens did not wish to have all her citizens turned out of the same mould, but, while giving equal opportunities to all, neither expected nor wished that every one should follow the same line or reach the same goal. Yet this liberty, allowed in practice, was not always in accordance with the theory, at least of individual thinkers: Plato, for instance, who was deeply influenced by Spartan ideals, attached the highest importance to the State, and though, in his *Republic,*[1] he would have the individuals highly trained in many branches of learning which in Sparta or early Rome would have been rejected as either superfluous or harmful, it has been often pointed out that the individuals in his State pass a laborious life of service and self-sacrifice in order to assure the greatest happiness to the greatest number; [2] while his strictures on poetry and other imitative arts shew further that the individual is to him of little importance.[3]

But the real contrast of principle between the Spartan and Athenian systems is that, while the former, having an eye always to practical matters, considered any kind of culture undesirable, the latter always placed it in the front among the qualifications for a good life. In this the Spartans were followed unconsciously by the old Romans: a Cincinnatus, when he was not leading an army or following the plough, did not trouble his head with literature; the only written works with which he was familiar were his farm accounts and the laws of the Twelve Tables.

The Spartan system of education may seem at first sight to be only of historical interest and of no value for the guidance of modern thought; yet a study of it had a deep influence on Plato, whose writings on educational theory have always commanded attention, and on Xenophon, who, though less read, has not been without his importance in the history of the subject. The old Roman system gradually gave place to new methods induced partly by contacts with Greek practice and partly by the study of Greek theory; but before it passed away it had left an indelible stamp on the character of the nation which insensibly evolved it. As a preliminary, therefore, to studying either the developed practice or advanced theory of Greece or of Rome in relation to their influence on subsequent ages, it is indispensable to pass these primitive systems under consideration.

It was not, however, the Athenian system, but the system developed in Hellenistic times, which directly influenced Rome. In the age of the successors of Alexander, cities such as Alexandria, Pergamum and Antioch rivalled, and to some extent eclipsed, Athens as centres of learning; so that Roman and Hellenistic education must be considered side by side. Under the Empire we shall have to consider not so much the form of education at Rome, as the wider aspect of a Graeco-Roman education extending over a great part of the civilized world. Even in the last generation of the Republic a considerable number of Romans of the upper classes had gone to Greece to complete their education — Horace, Cicero, and in particular Cicero's correspondent Atticus may be mentioned in this connection.[4] At a somewhat later period this system of what we may call University education became still more prevalent. The adoption by Rome of Christianity as the state-religion to some extent modified the course of education; but the study of the Greek and Latin languages never entirely died out, and the methods of instruction followed more or less the classical traditions. The end of the Middle Ages is characterized by the gradual secularization of education and its emancipation from ecclesiastical tradition. Its scope was widened by the inclusion of the natural sciences, whose study may be said to have begun with Roger Bacon, and of the Higher Mathematics, which in their applied form of Astronomy, had a long struggle for existence in the face of persecution, but emerged triumphant at the end. The complexity of modern educational systems owes but little directly to Greece and Rome; it is true, however, that the native literature of all countries has been built up to a great extent on a classical foundation, and this is inevitably due to the importance which has always been attached in the school-curricula to the ancient languages, which, to that extent, have never become ‘dead.’

Some analogies between modern and ancient method may be discerned, particularly in the three grades into which education is now generally divided. As Plato's theory carried the education of all citizens up to a certain point, reserving 'secondary' education for a smaller number and allowing fewer still to embark on the third stage, so we have now education of the mass of the population at an elementary stage; a continuation up to a higher age for selected pupils, and, finally, University courses for those who are thought fitted to carry those studies still further.

Our Universities themselves owe their form to the Universities of the Middle Ages, which were mainly of ecclesiastical origin and definitely anti-pagan in spirit; but those mediaeval institutions were closely analogous to the philosophical and rhetorical schools which they superseded, and owe a great deal to them in form if not in spirit.

The greatest revolution in School and University education is the modern introduction of technical training which will fit a man for a trade or business; this, as we shall see, is far removed from the classical spirit. The ideal of Athens, Sparta, and Republican Rome was to make a man a good citizen; in Imperial times the balance rather shifted towards culture for its own sake; the ideal of Elizabethan England was a combination of the two — to produce the cultured gentleman who should also be an able man of affairs. The idea of including in a general education any specialized training for trade or business is entirely modern.

I. SPARTA

I

DORIAN education is known to us from the systems prevailing in Sparta and Crete. Apart from some differences in detail, these systems are so closely similar that it will be sufficient for present purposes to fix our attention on Sparta.[1]

Sparta is an example, unique among Aryan races, of an important state highly organized on principles of scientific savagery. There have been in history other examples of military nations which, owing to economic pressure, have sought and conquered new lands, expelling some of the inhabitants and keeping the remainder temporarily in subjection. The early history of England is partly a record of successive conquests, by Saxons, Danes, and Normans, but the more important part of that history tells of the gradual assimilation of the interests of the conquerors and the conquered, and the fusion of the various races into a composite but uniform whole.

The Spartans, coming into Greece on the tide of the Dorian invasion, settled, like other invaders, in the land they had won, but, unlike immigrants elsewhere, they were never fused with the older population nor assimilated to their neighbours. They remained through the centuries as a garrison in conquered territory, intent only on preserving, not on widening, their boundaries. They abstained from trade and did not even hear the call of agriculture, such work as was necessary for the support of life under the simplest conditions being left to slaves. They were indifferent to literature; they neither developed any art of their own nor adopted that of others. Throughout their history clearly marked distinctions separated the three classes into which the inhabitants of Laconia were divided — the *Spartiatae,* the dominant race; the *Perioeci* or 'dwellers around,' who had lived in the land before the coming of the Dorians: these were free men, engaged in commerce and agriculture, and were liable for military service, but had no share in the government; and lastly the *Helots,* who were also natives of the land, but had been reduced to serfdom by the invaders. These serfs were treated for the most part cruelly and kept in subjection by brutal methods, but being a hardy race they attempted from time to time to revolt, and the Spartans lived in constant apprehension of a Helot rising.

The dominant class was but a small minority of the inhabitants, and of this minority only a small number were at any time concerned with government, for though there was an assembly of all male citizens over thirty years of age, it had little power or influence, all details of administration being managed by the two kings, and the council of twenty-eight elders, to whom at an early, but uncertain date, was added a board of five elected officers called *ephors* or overseers.

The form of the Spartan constitution, which was never modified except once, by the creation of the ephorate, was of immemorial antiquity, and was ascribed by the Spartans themselves to a half mythical legislator named Lycurgus, who was also credited with having instituted the educational system.[2]

Owing to the peculiar nature of the oligarchy under which they lived, the majority of Spartan citizens found that politics made very little demand on their time. Since, moreover, they were, as has been mentioned above, spared both the anxieties of trade and the fatigue of productive manual labour, they were free to devote nearly the whole of their energies to occupations more or less closely related to military training. Such parts of the day as could be spared from drill, hunting, and gymnastics were normally spent in the *leschai* or clubs, where conversation centred on the discussion of manly deeds and Spartan ideals of nobility in general. The men, at any rate those of the highest caste, took their meals in messes (*Phiditia*), and, until they reached the age of thirty, did not even go home to sleep. All life was organized on a military basis, and while in other communities war was regarded as a costly and unpleasant hindrance to the development of the peaceful arts, to Sparta a period of peace was useful only as giving more leisure for preparation in the arts of war.

2

SUCH being the national ideals, every child born was regarded as a recruit for the national army, and was subject to state-discipline from the beginning. New-born children were examined by the elders of the tribe to which their father belonged, and if they were found to be imperfect physically, or seemed to be of weakly constitution, they were exposed on the mountain-side, and left to die unless some of the Helots or of the Perioeci took pity on them.

All children were brought up by their mothers till the age of seven, though even before reaching that age boys sometimes went with their fathers to the men's dining-clubs, where they sat on the floor and listened to the men's talk. They apparently received food there, and possibly some special fare was provided for them. The ordinary Spartan diet, of broth and black bread, was so unpalatable as to give rise to the proverb that 'hunger is the best sauce.' Only violent exercise could give even the men an appetite for it, and a visitor introduced for a meal is said once to have remarked that he now understood why the Spartans did not fear death. At seven the boys were taken away from home and lived henceforward under regulations similar to those which governed the men. Each boy was assigned to an *ile* or division, and these *ilai* were grouped in larger units called *agelai* or *bouai* (herds). The boys of each *ile* lived together day and night. One boy of each division acted as a prefect; he was called *Bouagor* (herdsman) and had some disciplinary powers; the whole 'herd' was under an *Eiren*, a young man over twenty chosen for his courage and good moral character, and all the *agelai* were under the general control of a superintendent (*Paidonomos*), a citizen of rank and position. This officer had special attendants called 'whip-bearers,' whose office was no sinecure; in fact corporal punishments were both frequent and severe, and could be inflicted by any person in authority.[3]

Supervision did not end here, for every grown-up citizen had disciplinary powers over any boy whom he happened to meet, and such powers were frequently exercised. Thus repression was the general rule; unquestioning obedience under all circumstances was enforced by frequent and often brutal punishments, and there was no room for individuality, nor for initiative, except within the narrowest limits. The results of the system were far-reaching; taught always to obey, the Spartans were discouraged from independent thought and action. In the many centuries of her history Sparta produced innumerable good soldiers but very few great generals; and in politics, while she could govern herself, she had no idea of governing others.

The boys of each *agela* lived together under the superintendence of the *Eiren;* it was the duty of the older boys to gather firewood, and of the younger to supply vegetables. Such supplies could only be obtained by stealing, either from farms in the country or from the stores in the men's messes. Such theft, though punished severely if detected by the owners, was approved and encouraged as being a useful training for foraging in war. The system must have called for considerable ingenuity. Their simple meals were shared in common; they slept on rushes on the ground without bedclothes, and their dress in all seasons was a single rough garment. They were accustomed to go without shoes, and bathed daily, through summer and winter, in the river Eurotas.

The education was mainly physical; the formal part of it consisted of gymnastic and athletic exercises, graded according to the age of the pupils. The younger boys practised running, jumping, and ball playing, the older ones learned to throw the discus and the javelin, to box and to wrestle. These accomplishments were not an end in themselves, but were esteemed chiefly as a means of hardening the body, teaching the youth to bear pain and fatigue, and generally fostering such qualities of strength and endurance as would be valuable in war. Dancing, which was another integral part of the early training, served the same purpose: it seems to have consisted largely of war-dances, which imitated the actions and evolutions of the soldier, and was sometimes performed in full panoply, to the music of flutes. It had, however, a religious element also, as we hear of boys giving performances of dancing and gymnastics at certain festivals in honour of the gods.

Some attention was given to music, alone of the arts; the boys learned to sing solo or in chorus, certain selections from Homer being frequently chanted in unison, as well as some national songs, for instance those of the patriotic poet Tyrtaeus, who enjoyed great popularity in Sparta; the laws of Lycurgus also were learned by heart and recited; but beyond these meagre scraps it would appear that literary education was neglected. It is probable that most Spartans could read and write, but no mention is made of reading and writing as forming part of the state-education. Isocrates thought it unlikely that even the most intelligent Spartans would study his speeches, unless they could find someone to read them aloud, while, according to Plato, very few of them knew the elements of arithmetic.[4] Such statements as these may, no doubt, be discounted, but they point in general to a very low standard of education.

The physical training, as we have said, aimed at developing a good bodily condition in general rather than special excellence in any particular sport. The punishments inflicted on the boys were often disproportionately severe, in order that they might learn to endure pain; and this was so much the national ideal that boys on the verge of manhood voluntarily submitted, quite apart from the idea of punishment, to being flogged at the altar of Artemis Orthia, and, it is said, even practised beforehand for the ordeal, which was so severe that the victims sometimes died. Such an initiation-ceremony is unparalleled except in the annals of some Indian tribes.[5]

The spirit of pugnacity was encouraged by frequent fights between individual boys, which were often instigated by their elders, though they might be stopped if they went too far. Among the youths there were organized games which were more like battles without weapons; two teams met on a level plain, and the object of each was to drive the other, by any available physical means, into the river. Even the full-grown men were encouraged to fight by an extraordinary institution of Lycurgus: the ephors selected three men in the prime of life out of the whole body of the citizens. Each of these three *hippagretai* (masters of the horse) selected a hundred others, declaring in public why he chose this one and rejected that one; thus there were formed three companies of jealous rivals, ready to fight whenever and wherever they met, and with this prospect before them they were bound to keep constantly in training.[6] Those who had passed their prime were encouraged to spend all their spare time in hunting.

3

THE SPARTANS themselves were divided into two social classes, the *Homoioi* or 'Peers,' who were members of the Phiditia, and the *Hypomeiones*, 'Inferiors,' who owing, probably, to inability to pay their contributions to the mess, had dropped out. There is some evidence for believing that the national education above described was normally restricted to the sons of Peers, i.e., to boys who might expect eventually to join the messes to which their fathers belonged. Sometimes, however, other boys were admitted on the introduction of a Peer, who wished to have them as school-companions for his own sons, and was willing to be responsible for them and pay their expenses. Occasionally foreigners were admitted; at any rate it appears that Xenophon, a thorough admirer of Lacedaemonian institutions, had his own sons brought up in Sparta; but more often they were either sons of distinguished *perioeci* or belonged to the class of *mothakes*, illegitimate sons of Spartans by Helot mothers. But boys other than the sons of Spartans of the highest rank, although admitted to the privileges of education, were seldom raised to the rank of citizenship.[7]

It would seem, then, that the education here described was intended primarily for the children of the upper classes, though a few others were, under exceptional circumstances, allowed to share in it. What the lot of the lower classes of Lacedaemonians was, we cannot even conjecture, except that, as we know they were called on for military service, they must have had a physical education similar to that of the Spartiatae, and this must have been organized by the State; but that there was no public education for them in even the rudiments of letters or arts is probable from the silence of all authorities.

4

LYCURGUS, according to Plutarch, had some views on the physical, though not the political, equality of the sexes; he held that wool-work was a more suitable occupation for slaves than for free women, and that women, just as much as men, should aim at physical perfection, which could only be reached by careful training. He valued physical beauty only by eugenic standards — woman's highest ideal was motherhood, and a fine race could be maintained only if the women as well as the men reached a high standard of physical fitness. Accordingly he ordained that girls as well as boys should be brought up to an open-air life and accustomed to athletic exercises. The girls lived at home, but they had gymnasia of their own in which they practised among themselves running, jumping, and wrestling, and they also learned to throw the discus and javelin. They were taught, like the boys, to swim and to ride, and at the festival of Hyacinthia they raced on horseback. Their training in these exercises was entirely apart from that of the boys, but on some occasions they danced in company with the latter. One outcome of this cult of the body was that the Spartan women had a reputation throughout Greece for beauty, and they seem, as a class, to have developed an independence of character far in advance of their contemporaries in other states, for instance, Athens, where girls were mostly occupied with home duties. In literary and artistic education they were probably at least as deficient as their brothers.

5

In modern times those countries which have to submit to compulsory military training regard it as a serious interruption to education, but in the case of Sparta, where all education was but a preparation for war, it was reasonable to follow the system to its conclusion. The Spartan youth, between the ages of eighteen and twenty, already trained to discipline and the use of arms, were enrolled in the *Crypteia*, a secret organization conducted on military lines and under the leadership of an older man. Their chief duty was to patrol the country in small detachments, sleeping in the open and avoiding observation as much as possible, and to keep watch on the Helots, observing particularly any signs of an independent spirit or self-assertiveness which might seem to indicate an intention to revolt. Individual Helots who shewed signs of becoming too prominent as leaders of opinion among their fellows, or were overheard in any treasonable utterance, were reported by individual spies to the leader of the troop, who, if the case seemed serious, might take action solely on this information. The victim was then removed by assassination. Killing in this case was no murder since, by the forethought of the government, war was annually declared against the Helots to cover any such contingencies.[8]

The severest indictment of the Spartan system of training is uttered by Aristotle, who, writing at a time when the power of Sparta was no longer predominant, could see things from a proper perspective. "It is well known," he tells us, "that the Spartans, while they attended to their laborious drill, were superior to all others, but now they are beaten by others both in war and gymnastics: for their superiority depended not on their method of training the youths, but on the fact that they trained them while others did not. We must judge the Spartans not by what they were, but by what they are; for now they have rivals in education, while formerly they had none." [9]

II. ATHENS

I

WE HAVE seen that Spartan education was regulated by the state, and was designed to train citizens to serve their country. It may be called vocational, since its chief object was to prepare the boys for military service. Athenian education, on the other hand, was almost entirely individualistic; its object was the training of character and taste, and though by custom it developed into a more or less uniform system, this system was not imposed by any law, nor indeed was education in any form prescribed or regulated by the state. It owed its organization solely to private enterprise; anybody might set up a school, and there was no restriction as to the subjects which might be taught. Although there were no state-schools, from early times there were laws regulating the conduct of the numerous private establishments. Aeschines ascribes to Solon (594 B.C.) the framing of regulations concerning the hours at which schools should open and close, the number of boys who might attend each school, the school-age, and so on.[1] There is some further evidence of the existence of organized education both on the mainland of Greece and elsewhere in Greek lands in comparatively early times. Herodotus records a disaster caused by the collapse of a school building in Chios in 494 B.C.[2] When, in 480 B.C., the Athenians were forced to abandon their homes before the Persian War was over, the people of Troezen not only gave them shelter but paid the children's school-fees.[3] In the Periclean age Anaxagoras the philosopher left a sum of money to his native town, Clazomenae, on condition that the anniversary of his death should be celebrated as a school-holiday.[4] By the time of the Peloponnesian war (431–404 B.C.), Boeotia, usually regarded as a backward country, had schools even in the small towns, for Thucydides records with horror the action of a horde of barbarian mercenaries who forced their way into Mycalessus and, entering the largest school in the town, murdered all the boys.[5]

2

In the third century we hear for the first time of the definite endowment of schools — not, it is true, in Greece itself, but in Asia Minor. Chance has preserved, and archaeological research has recently recovered for us, an inscription recording the gift, on the part of one Eudemus, of a large sum of money for the perpetual endowment of a school for the sons of the free citizens at Miletus, where a decree of the people provides machinery for the appointment of a sort of school-council who shall be responsible for the administration of the funds, the appointment of teachers, and the general management of the institution.[6] The decree also fixed the salaries to be paid to the masters, and it is noticeable that these were very small, viz., thirty drachmas a month for physical instructors and forty for elementary teachers, which must have been hardly a living wage. At Athens in the fifth century the payment of sailors in the fleet was in some cases as high as a drachma a day, i.e., twenty-nine or thirty a month, and if we consider the probable rise in the price of commodities in the interval, we must carry the impression that school-teaching was not, at Miletus, a lucrative business. In Teos, where we have some information of a similar nature, the rate of salary was higher, the master of the highest class getting six hundred drachmas a year, and two others five hundred and fifty and five hundred respectively.[7]

3

THE SCHOOLS of the classical period were, as we have seen, organized by private enterprise, receiving neither recognition nor support from the state, though from early times they appear (*supra*, p. 25) to have been subject to certain regulations. The master supported himself and paid his assistants out of the fees of the pupils, which were paid monthly. The scholastic profession seems to have been held in little respect, though it is true that our evidence is slight and not always trustworthy. There is a story that Alcibiades beat a schoolmaster, on the ground that he did not possess a copy of Homer; but the tale is not well authenticated, nor could such conduct anyhow be taken as typical.[8] Demosthenes ridiculed his rival Aeschines for being the son of a schoolmaster and having himself been an assistant in the school. "As a boy," he writes, "you helped your father by performing menial offices in the school, grinding the ink and sweeping out the waiting-room." [9] And, again, a comic poet says of a lost friend: "He is either dead or a schoolmaster by now;" [10] but such jibes need not be taken too seriously. In modern times the Schoolmaster is, like the Professor, frequently a butt of the comic papers, providing mirth for the ignorant, and even distinguished masters in well-known schools have been known to refer with scant respect to their own profession and to themselves as representatives of it.

Athenian school-education was divided into two stages, the elementary, from the age of six to that of fourteen, the secondary, from fourteen to eighteen, while at eighteen all Athenian youths entered on a modified kind of military training which lasted for two years. This consisted of a service in the *peripoloi* or frontier-guard, in the course of which the young men, under the superintendence of senior officers, were, after some preliminary training at Athens, stationed at some one of the fortresses round Attica. If we may judge from a private speech of Demosthenes the training was not severe and the discipline was lax. The youths, when not on duty, expended their superfluous energy on skylarking and practical jokes. A young Athenian thus describes his experiences: [11] "I went out two years ago to Panakton, where we were detailed for garrison-duty. The sons of Conon had a tent near to ours, to my great discomfort. They used to start drinking after breakfast, and continued it throughout the day, persisting in this practice all the time of our service. So by the time that the rest of us had fixed for dinner they were already drunk, and playing tricks, first on our servants and eventually on us. They would assert that the servants engaged in cooking let the smoke blow in their faces, or were insolent, and on this or any other pretext they thrashed them and emptied the slop-buckets over their heads. Though annoyed at such conduct, we at first put it from our minds, but when they persisted in using abusive language to us, the whole of the mess went and complained to the general in command."

The complainant goes on to relate how, in spite of a severe reprimand from the commanding officer, the offenders not only continued in their offensive conduct but resorted to open violence, which caused a free fight in camp and brought all the officers out of their tents. The fact that this was the only military service to which the Athenian was normally subject in time of peace points a marked contrast to the Spartan system, under which all the life of a citizen was spent in preparation for war.

School-education was entirely voluntary, but was nevertheless almost universal. A knowledge of literature was traditional in the old aristocratic families, and when democracy developed in Athens the people were quick to realize the importance of education, and generally gave their sons the best which they could afford. The elementary schools, and the higher grade schools when they came into existence, confined themselves to literary, musical, and gymnastic instruction. There was no organized training in practical arts or sciences, as indeed, until very recent times, was the case in the modern world. The Greeks in general regarded handicrafts and trades as vulgar, and unworthy of a free man. Aristotle condemns such trades as interfere with bodily or mental development; [12] Xenophon harps on the same string, adding that tradesmen have less leisure for serving the State;[13] Plato considers tradesmen unfit to be citizens.[14] Large numbers of the poorer citizens at Athens were, however, forced to do something for their living. Socrates was the son of a statuary, and himself worked at the craft, nor was he on that account excluded from the society of the rich and aristocratic classes. Trades were, as in this case, largely hereditary, though apprenticeship was not uncommon.[15] Such technical training comes in for only casual mention, and is not regarded by any Greek theorist as forming part of education.

We must further note that there was no organization, either public or private, for the education of girls; though we can hardly believe that the majority of Athenian women were entirely illiterate, such references as we have to women's education imply the belief that a knowledge of housekeeping was all that could be reasonably expected of a girl up to the time of her marriage.[16]

4

TRADITIONALLY, Athenian education was divided into two branches: *μουσική*, the training of the mind, and *γυμναστική*, the training of the body. These words, commonly transliterated as ‘ music ’ and ‘ gymnastic,’ give a wrong impression, for music, though important, was not indispensable, the most important element in the training of the mind being literature; and ‘ gymnastic ’ comprised not only the regulated exercise which we understand by gymnastics, but games and other physical activities in general.

School-life began for the Athenian boy at the age of six or seven, when he was sent to the school selected, under the conduct of a trustworthy slave called the *παιδαγωγός*, whose duty it was to watch him carefully on the way and keep him under surveillance all day. *Paedagogi* were not in any way concerned with teaching, but they were responsible for the behaviour and moral conduct of their charges, and therefore, at any rate in earlier times, elderly slaves of good manners, trustworthy character, and some education were chosen. Thus Sikinnos, the paedagogus of Themistocles’ sons, was entrusted by his master with an important mission, namely the carrying of a famous message to Xerxes before the battle of Salamis; [17] and from literature, e.g., the *Medea* of Euripides, we gather that such slaves often held an important place in the household and stood high in their masters' esteem.[18]

The school-day began at sunrise. Solon, if we may trust Aeschines, had made it unlawful for schools to open before day-break or to remain open after dark, on the ground that in the night-hours the boys might meet undesirable characters and be exposed to corrupting influences.[19] Soon after dawn, then, the boy had to get up, and after a light breakfast would start to walk to school, accompanied by the paedagogus, who carried his writing-tablets and books, and also his lyre, if it was the day for a music lesson.

The morning hours were divided between ordinary school-lessons and games or other physical exercise; the boy went home for dinner, but returned to school shortly afterwards, to spend the afternoon, up to sunset, in much the same way as the morning had been passed.[20] Exactly how the hours were divided between mental and physical training we do not know, but evidently the latter occupied a considerable part of the boy's time. A school-day, then, was long and exhausting, and there was no time or opportunity for homework. There were no Sundays to give a weekly day of rest to both masters and pupils, but religious festivals were observed as holidays, and gave a welcome, and fairly frequent, relief to all. In the month of Anthesterion (February–March) these days of festival were numerous, and Theophrastus (third century B.C.) describes the 'mean man' as not sending his children to school at all during this month, because he feels that he will not get his money's worth.[21]

The furniture of the schoolroom was of the simplest, consisting of a high chair for the master and stools or benches for the boys. In writing, the boys rested the tablets on their knees, as there were no desks. Writing was taught by means of copies, inscribed on the wax-coated tablets with a stilus, — at any rate in the fifth century. In the fourth century Demosthenes explicitly refers to ink being used in schools, the writing instrument being in that case a reed-pen.[22]

As a preliminary to reading, the names of the letters were first learned, sometimes by means of a metrical alphabet, of which a specimen is preserved in Athenaeus.[23] The children were next taught to combine consonants and vowels and learn the resultant sounds. The same writer gives us an example of a class divided into two semi-choruses, of which the first will chant βῆτα, ἄλφα, βα, and so on with the rest of the vowels, and the second half will take up the burden with γάμμα, ἄλφα, γα, and so on. The next stage was to learn the forms of the letters, and this was followed by instruction in the component parts of a sentence.[24] At a somewhat later stage came writing from dictation, and almost from the beginning the children had to learn by heart and recite chosen passages of poetry. Owing to the scarcity of books the passages to be recited would often be dictated by the master.

Simple lessons in arithmetic consisted of counting first on the fingers, and then with pebbles. The abacus was a counting-board containing grooves in which pebbles or counters could be inserted, the value of each depending on the groove in which it was placed. Owing to the primitive and inconvenient systems of notation employed by the Greeks, a system still more cumbrous than that of the Romans, even simple sums could not be done on paper by the methods which the introduction of Arabic numerals has made possible for us, while in dealing with large numbers some mechanical device such as the abacus was indispensable. We must note, however, that the abacus, by assigning different values according to the position of the counters, prepared the way for the modern system of numerical notation according to the decimal principle.[25]

Boys at Athens were encouraged to learn by heart great masses of poetry, particularly Homer and Hesiod, but also Simonides and the gnomic poets. A character in Xenophon assures us that he knew the whole of the *Iliad* and the *Odyssey* by heart.[26] Having learned their lessons, the pupils were made to recite long passages with appropriate delivery and gesture. Musical instruction began at a later stage than the 'grammatical'; and the object again was a moral one; music had a moral value in itself and also was indispensable to the proper understanding and interpretation of the lyric poets.

Physical instruction began at an early age, the boys being taken by their paedagogi at certain hours to the *palaestrae,* where the trainer (παιδοτρίβης) superintended their exercises in running, jumping, and wrestling. Swimming was a regular recreation, and dancing, which also had a religious aspect, was one of the most important parts of the physical training.

5

THIS curriculum, consisting only of reading and writing, a little simple arithmetic, and much repetition of poetry, combined with the necessary amount of simple music and graduated physical exercises, was continued in most cases to the age of fourteen or thereabouts, and was found sufficient for all classes in the early days of Athenian history. The triumph of Greece over the Persian invaders in 480–479 B.C. gave a great impulse to expansion and development of all kinds; the formation of the Confederacy of Delos brought Athens into closer contact with the Greek cities of Ionia which, under the influence of Oriental civilization, had far outstripped the cities of the mainland in culture and material prosperity. The great increase of wealth in Attica due to the growth of foreign trade produced a leisured class capable of assimilating and improving on this colonial civilization. Athenian energy found its proper outlet in the intellectual and artistic energies of the Periclean age. Boys of the well-to-do classes, who were not under the necessity of working for a living, required something to occupy their minds between the elementary school stage and the time when the State would require their service in the ranks of the *peripoloi*, and schools of a higher grade came into being to meet the growing needs of the population. The courses of study followed depended entirely on the individual taste of the parents, who probably made arrangements with private teachers of special subjects; and our knowledge of both systems is very scanty. We hear in a spurious Platonic dialogue of Socrates visiting the school of Dionysius and finding a class of boys discussing a problem in astronomy.[27] The boy Theaetetus, in Plato's dialogue of that name, describes a lesson in advanced arithmetic and geometry at which he had recently been present.[28] The Grammatistae, the instructors in such schools, dealt also with literary subjects, especially the interpretation and appreciation of poetry.[29] This would prepare the way for the more advanced instruction given at a later stage by the Sophists. Geography was also studied to some extent, and Aristotle mentions and approves of drawing as a school-subject.[30]

As in Rome at a later date, so at Athens in the fifth century there were some who deplored the passing away of old ideals. Aristophanes, speaking through one of his characters, describes the old-fashioned education: " First of all boys had to be seen and not heard; the boys of each ward had to march together to the lyre-school, without overcoats, even though it snowed. They were taught to sing the fine old national songs, and if one of them played the fool or tried any flourishes such as modern musicians use, he was thrashed for disrespect to the Muses. At meals children were not allowed to grab dainties from in front of their elders, or giggle or cross their legs. This was the training that produced the heroes of Marathon." [31]

6

TO THE extent already indicated, some instruction in instrumental music was normally included in the school course, the lessons being given by a *citharistes* or lyrist, but whether at his own house or in the general school is uncertain. The Greeks attached great importance to the influence of music in the development of the character, special attention being paid to rhythm as likely to help in the formation of orderly habits, and, so far as the fifth century is concerned, we know definitely that it was on these grounds that music was studied.[32] It was never intended or even thought desirable that the citizen youth should attain a degree of proficiency which would put him on a level with the professionals; public performance, both in music and in dancing, was left to a different class of artists.[33] It appears, however, that in the fourth century there was a change in the Athenian attitude towards music, which, according to Aristotle, was now sometimes studied for pleasure,[34] and this he thinks the only rational object. Aristotle, though he does not ignore the moral influence of music, refers to Homer as a proof that music was invented for man's enjoyment. He would admit it into a scheme of education, but only on sufferance. "Children must have something to do, and the rattle of Archytas, which people give to children to occupy them and prevent them from breaking things in the house, was a fine invention, for young things cannot keep still. Musical education is a rattle for bigger children."[35]

Socrates, in Plato's *Protagoras,* strongly emphasizes the moral aspect of education. After laying great stress on the importance of early home training, he continues: "At a later stage they (the parents) send the boy to teachers, instructing them to see to his manners even more than to his reading and music. . . When the boy has learned his letters they put into his hands the works of great poets, and in these are contained many admonitions, tales, praises, and encomia of ancient famous men, which he is required to learn by heart, in order that he may imitate or emulate them and desire to become like them. The teachers of the lyre take similar care that their pupil is temperate and gets into no mischief; and when they have taught him the use of the lyre they introduce him to the works of the lyric poets, which they set to music, and make their tunes and rhythms familiar to the children's souls, in order that they may be more gentle and harmonious and rhythmical, for the life of man in every part has need of harmony and rhythm." [36] On reading this extract from the *Protagoras* we cannot fail to be impressed by the importance which Socrates attaches to the moral purpose of education. This was not a peculiarity of Socrates; the Athenian ideal was that education should be ethical rather than intellectual. The quality most to be desired in a boy was modesty, and the whole course of training both at home and in school was designed to foster this quality. Every care was taken to protect a boy from corrupting influences: he must not go out at night when evil characters were abroad; on his way to school the paedagogus must keep him from bad company; he must not attend the performance of a comedy; he might go out with his father to a dinner-party, but he was sent home early, before the progress of the festivities had caused any relaxation in the manners of his elders. In the company of older people he must not speak unless spoken to, and whether at home or out of doors he must preserve a modest and unobtrusive demeanour. We have a picture of a typical well-behaved boy in Plato's *Theaetetus*, who is modest in his bearing towards his elders, quick of apprehension, and eager to learn.[37] Modesty and respect for elders were two of the qualities which Aristophanes thought specially desirable in the young.[38] Xenophon's hero, Cyrus the Elder, was represented by him as a pattern of modesty: "As he began to grow up, he talked less and in gentler tones; he was so bashful that he blushed whenever he came into the presence of his elders."[39] We may quote another instance, from Xenophon's *Banquet*. The young

Autolycus having won a contest for boys in the Panathenaic festival, he and his father were invited to dinner by his father's friend Callias. In the course of the evening each guest had to state what was the thing on which he most prided himself: the answers were in some cases serious, but more often spoken in jest. Someone suggested that the boy, doubtless, was most proud of his prize; but Autolycus, blushing as he spoke, answered for himself: "Certainly not." Someone asked then: "What is it you are proud of, Autolycus?" "Of my father," replied the lad, and leaned closer towards him.[40] Even in so late a writer as Lucian we find the same feeling. This is his account of the school-boy: "He gets up at dawn, washes the sleep from his eyes, pins his cloak over his shoulders, and goes out from home with downcast eyes, not looking any of the passers-by in the face."[41] . . . This is the kind of character which Aristophanes admired, though he believed it to be passing away.

7

AT EIGHTEEN the young Athenian ceased to be regarded as a boy, and was enrolled in the ranks of the *Ephebi,* who, at any rate during one period of the city's history, underwent a compulsory military training.

Our knowledge of the activities of the Ephebi is unfortunately scanty. It cannot be proved that there was in the fifth century any real organization for the training of the young men when first enrolled on the list of citizens at the age of eighteen. The earliest literary reference to what is sometimes called the 'Ephebic College' is in the pseudo-Platonic dialogue *Axiochus,* generally attributed to Aeschines the Socratic, though it is sometimes held that Thucydides' references to the *νεώτατοι*, the youngest class of soldiers, whom he contrasts with the older men past the normal military age, imply the existence of some such body.[42] Aristotle's *Constitution of Athens* devotes a chapter to their training at the end of the fourth century B.C., and the earliest of numerous inscriptions in which they are mentioned dates from 333 B.C.[43] At this time there were 1000 Ephebi, but the numbers very rapidly declined, until in 276 B.C. only twenty-nine from all the Athenian tribes were enrolled. This discrepancy cannot be explained by the decline in population. The numbers establish almost with certainty the hypothesis that whereas, in the beginning, service was compulsory for all members of the first three political classes, at a later date it became voluntary, and further, that about the same time foreigners began to be admitted. We know that in imperial Roman times the foreigners many times outnumbered the Athenians in this body. During the fourth century, it seems that military service was compulsory for youths of the citizen class between the ages of eighteen and twenty. The first year was devoted to instruction in the City; during the second, the partially trained bands were sent, under senior men as officers, to garrison-duty in certain frontier-posts, though on some stated occasions they were recalled to Athens for the purposes of a general review.

Towards the end of the fourth century the service ceased to be compulsory, and its length was reduced to one year. In the second century, when Athens was no longer of political importance, intellectual studies were introduced which gradually superseded military training. Under the general guidance of an official called *Sophronistes*, the young men attended in the gymnasia lectures by philosophers, rhetoricians, and grammarians. Thus the whole character of the institution was changed: in the beginning it had a democratic basis and was purely military; in the end it was neither military nor even national, but had become a club for rich young men of Athens and other states, devoted mostly to education of the kind from which, by considerations of expense, the lower classes were inevitably debarred.

8

No organization, either public or private, provided for the carrying of any of the above-mentioned studies beyond the school-age; but Athens acquired during the fifth century a thirst for higher education, and this was satisfied to some extent at first by the Sophists and later, from the fourth century onwards, by the philosophical Schools. The Sophists were certain professional educators, mostly coming either from the Greek colonies in Asia Minor and that part of Italy known as Magna Graecia. They were individuals of various interests whom it was found convenient to class under the same title, but they must not be regarded as forming any organized body or representing any common opinions. As opposed to the various philosophers who had from time to time sought after knowledge for its own sake and expounded their systems to chosen disciples, the Sophists were for the most part frankly sceptical. They professed only to impart such teaching as could fit a man to take his proper place in the ranks of citizens and statesmen, and they travelled from town to town giving lectures and taking small classes of such young men as were able to pay their fees. These fees were sometimes high. Aristippus demanded one thousand drachmae for a course; [44] Isocrates required the same fee, and when Demosthenes offered two hundred for the fifth part of the course, Isocrates replied: " I can't cut my course into slices; the finest fish are sold whole." [45] Some earnest students made great sacrifices in order to profit by such instruction, even working in mills by night in order to raise the necessary fees for the classes held by day.[46]

Two lines of development may be traced in the Sophistry of the fifth and fourth centuries B.C , the Rhetorical and the Literary. The former begins with the Sicilian rhetoricians, Tisias and Corax, who taught the art of rhetoric at Syracuse. Another Western Greek, Gorgias of

Leontini, made forensic rhetoric an important element in education; he first became prominent as a teacher in Sicily, but after 427 B.C. he frequently visited Athens and other cities of central Greece. His importance lies chiefly in the influence which his writings had on the development of prose style, but as a forerunner of Isocrates, the inventor and user of 'Political Philosophy' as a means of education, he deserves to be mentioned here.

Of the Sophists more generally so called Protagoras of Abdera (*c.* 480–410 B.C.) was the first and greatest. He professed himself a teacher of 'virtue,' by which he meant not orthodox morality but those qualities which will fit a man to play worthily his part in public life. He was himself a man of wide education and sympathies, and had in him none of the qualities which we usually connote by the word 'sophistical.' He travelled for forty years or more about Greece, residing for several periods at Athens, and winning brilliant success by his lectures. The basis of his instruction was a comprehensive treatment of literature, for he held that a good general education is the best equipment that a man can have for public life. Plato, who was opposed on principle to the Sophists, treats him everywhere with respect, and vividly describes the excitement which the news of his arrival created among the young men of the upper classes at Athens.

Socrates relates how one morning before daybreak Hippocrates beat at his door, and rushed in as soon as it was opened, shouting, at the top of his voice, "Protagoras has come."[47] He knew the great Sophist only by reputation, and wished Socrates to introduce him; he could hardly be restrained from starting at once, but Socrates prevailed on him to wait for daylight. They therefore walked and conversed for a time in the courtyard, and in the course of the talk Socrates ascertained that what the young man wanted was not a professional but a general education — a sequel, in fact, to what he had learned at school. Arriving at the house of Callias, where Protagoras was staying, they found the latter already walking about in the cloisters, accompanied by a crowd of disciples, mostly foreigners, "whom he leads from city to city, holding them by the spell of his voice, like a second Orpheus;" and a distinguished company of well-known Athenians had already begun to assemble, including Critias, Alcibiades, and two sons of Pericles.

Somewhat later in time than Protagoras came Prodicus of Ceos, Euenos of Paros, and Hippias of Elis. Of these, Prodicus still gave to literature the chief place, though he also lectured on ethical principles; of Euenos little is known; Hippias attempted to impart to his pupils 'polymathy,' popular knowledge on all subjects, which would be sufficient for general purposes. He broadened education so much that it could have but little depth, and his successors, Euthydemus and Dionysodorus, not illogically, went farther still, and professed to teach a method of disputation, armed with which their pupils could dispense with knowledge altogether and, like journalists, discourse or argue on any subject under the sun without preparation.

9

THE SOPHISTS one and all were thorough-going sceptics, regarding philosophy as a futile struggle to attain knowledge of what was unknowable. Protagoras himself was the author of the famous dictum "Man is the measure of all things," and others followed him in holding that absolute truth was unattainable. They were not, however, conspirators against morality: they merely professed to teach what they described as 'Virtue,' that is, the quality which will enable a man to make a success of life, especially public life in a City-state. Their aims were frankly utilitarian.

Socrates, who is classed with them by Aristophanes,[48] though he himself repudiated the connection, was, like them, interested in Virtue, but differed from them in the interpretation of the term, which to him had a definite moral significance, namely the quality which will lead to right action, rather than successful action.

His theory of education was based upon a reasoned scepticism. Holding, like the Sophists, that knowledge is beyond our grasp, he maintained that 'opinions' are good or bad according as they are more or less serviceable when translated into action. He held that, though it is impossible to teach men Virtue, we may by certain processes substitute a right opinion for a wrong opinion. To know what was right, inevitably, to his mind, led to doing what was right; his aim was right conduct rather than success in life, and in order to lead men, if not to knowledge, at least to the opinion which would cause them to act rightly, he evolved the 'dialectical' or Socratic method of teaching. His method was, by means of searching interrogations of his pupil or listener, to clear away all loose definitions and arrive at a definite idea of what was meant by abstract terms, such as Justice, Virtue, and the like. In this 'dialectic' the pupil had to make as much effort as the teacher — a very different procedure from the long and formal discourses of the Sophists.

Socrates believed that he had a divine mission to be an educator, his duty being to lead men to clear thinking. About the details of ordinary school education he did not trouble himself. Two features in his teaching are, however, important in the history of Greek education — his insistence on the moral side, and the method of which he was the inventor. Practically all that we know about him is to be gathered from the works of his two disciples, Xenophon and Plato. The former, though an honest recorder, was not subtle enough always to understand the working of the master's mind, while the latter often used Socrates merely as a figure-head in the dialogues, attributing to him opinions and interests, e.g., in connection with abstruse philosophical questions, which the real Socrates certainly never entertained. Both, however, were deeply influenced by Socrates' ethical aims, and Plato elaborated and applied to his own purposes the dialectical method. Finally Isocrates, the last and greatest of the Sophists, himself at one time a pupil of Gorgias, established a school of political rhetoric and a system of political philosophy which was holding the field when Plato returned to Athens and founded the Academy.

10

PLATO for the last forty years of his life was accustomed to converse with his pupils in his own house, near the grove of Academus. On his death (347 B.C.) he bequeathed his estate to his nephew Speusippus, who, in turn, left it to his pupils. The Lyceum, the headquarters of the followers of Aristotle, had, similarly, private property in trust; the Epicurean school began its work in the gardens of Epicurus, which property was held by that philosopher's followers for some time; the Stoics alone seem to have possessed no property; but all these four schools were brotherhoods whose object was the acquisition of knowledge and its transmission to their pupils. Provision was made in every case for the succession to the headship on the death or retirement of the principal. To these four great schools came pupils from all parts of the Greek world in search of a higher education, more systematic and more permanent than in the earlier days could be obtained from the Sophists. Owing to their influence Athens continued, at least till the beginning of the Christian era, to be the centre of philosophical instruction, and the members of these schools, or their direct successors, were responsible for the bulk of the philosophical and a considerable portion of the scientific learning of the ancient world [49] down to the time of the closing of the philosophical schools and the confiscation of their property by the rescript of Justinian in 529 A.D.

II

THE ESTABLISHMENT of the philosophical schools of Athens, each having definite provision for the succession to the headship and a fixed place for meetings of teachers and pupils, has been regarded as marking the beginning of

University life in Greece. The conquests of Alexander, however, began a new phase in Greek history. Though he, like his father, Philip, had a great esteem for Athens — an esteem that was shared by many of his successors — it was inevitable that the conquest and settlement of the East should cause a shifting in the centre of gravity of civilization. In 332 B.C., during Alexander's lifetime, Alexandria was founded, destined soon to become a centre of learning with resources and opportunities such as Athens had never possessed.

The Museum of Alexandria, founded by Ptolemy Soter (d. 283 B.C.) and enriched and enlarged by his son and successor, Ptolemy Philadelphus (d. 247 B.C.), was an institute for learned men, founded and endowed primarily not for teaching, but for purposes of research. Here in the third century B.C. literature, mathematics, astronomy, mechanics, anatomy, and natural history were scientifically studied. The advantages of the great library and other facilities put in the way of higher learning attracted scholars and scientists from all parts of the Greek world. Here they lived a collegiate life, having a common hall for meals and enjoying the amenities of cloisters and gardens like those occupied by the philosophic schools at Athens. Closely connected with the Museum was the Library, which by the first century B.C. contained over half a million volumes. To Alexandria we owe the first attempts at scientific criticism of literature; a great output of poetry, which exercised an enormous and fatal influence on the form and content of Roman literature; and invaluable contributions to such sciences as mathematics, astronomy, medicine, and natural history. Other centres of learning rose to distinction shortly after Alexandria — notably Pergamum in Asia Minor, which by the end of the third century B.C. possessed a library of which Alexandria grew jealous;[50] and Antioch, where the patronage of the Seleucid dynasty established a Museum and Library. Other places of lesser, but yet considerable, importance were Pella, Cos, and Rhodes.

Athens meanwhile had lost all political influence, but continued to live on her reputation as the traditional home of learning. The Macedonians and other nations of the East fell under her spell, and even the Romans, when they came into close contact with Greece in the second century, succumbed to the same charm. Having unfortunately taken part in the First Mithridatic War, the city was besieged and captured by Sulla (86 B.C.), who massacred a large number of the inhabitants, cut down the trees of the Academy and Lyceum, and damaged the famous buildings. In the course of the next generation Athens had once more recovered a semblance of her old greatness; she became a favourite resort of Romans who were travelling in pursuit of culture, and thus directed the general flow of education in late Republican and Imperial times. In fact, from this period onwards, apart from differences of language, the educational systems of East and West followed the same channel.

III. GREEK THEORY

A. PLATO [427–347 B.C.]

I

THE CHIEF writers on educational theory among the Greeks of the Classical Age were Plato, Xenophon, Aristotle, and Isocrates; of these, the first two were strongly influenced by Spartan ideals and therefore to some extent reactionary.

Plato's educational theories are set forth in the *Republic,* a work of his maturity, and the *Laws,* the work of his old age, in which many of his former ideals are rejected as impracticable. It must always be borne in mind that the philosopher's chief aim in the *Republic* is the imaginary construction of a perfect State, and to this end the individual must to some extent be sacrificed, since his existence is only to be justified in so far as he is a useful member of the community. In the complete subordination of the wishes, and indeed the comfort, of the individual to the State's well-being we may trace Spartan influence, as also in some details of the physical education prescribed. But here the analogy ends, for whereas Sparta has only strength, the ideal State has in addition intelligence in the highest possible degree, and is indeed strong chiefly because of its intelligence. Perfection of the whole implies perfection of the parts, and so all members of the Republic must be educated up to the limit of their capacity in order that in their several grades they may perform their duties in the most intelligent and efficient way.[1]

2

In Plato's State the population is divided into three classes — the rulers, who are philosophers and responsible for the theory and practice of government; the guardians, a military caste, who safeguard the community; and the common people — husbandmen, artisans, tradesmen and the like, who provide the material necessaries of existence. With the lowest class Plato is hardly concerned; they are necessary for the existence of the community, but have few, if any, civic rights, and their education is of little importance, provided that they learn enough to enable them to carry on satisfactorily the business to which they are assigned. Plato does not expressly exclude them from the benefits of elementary education, and therefore we may assume that he would allow them to participate in it. He distinguishes three stages of education.[2] The first, which is perhaps intended for all citizens, is in general the same as the conventional education of all Athenian children, consisting of music for the mind and gymnastic for the body, though Plato points out that both branches are really for the benefit of the soul. 'Music,' of course, includes literature and humane culture in general as opposed to scientific training. Its study precedes that of 'gymnastic.' Boys and girls are to be educated together. The most careful attention must be paid to the surroundings in which the children are brought up; nothing mean or ugly must meet the eye or ear. Consequently the fairy tales of childhood must be under a strict censorship — a subject to which we shall recur later.

The ages at which various studies are to be begun are not mentioned in the *Republic,* but in the *Laws* we hear that children are to go to school at ten and spend three years in learning to read and write, and three more years in the study of 'music.' At the age of seventeen mental studies are broken off, and give place to a systematic physical training which lasts till the age of twenty, and corresponds roughly to the training of the Ephebi at Athens.

At this stage, if not before, the common people have passed out of sight, but, as Plato contemplated the possibility of a youth rising by special merit from a lower class to a higher, just as the reverse process may take place — a soldier, for instance, who shews cowardice, is degraded to the ranks of the artisans — we must assume that in exceptional cases the son of an artisan may have been singled out for education to this point and beyond. Certainly at the age of twenty some selection is made,[3] and those who are worthy spend ten years in the study of the sciences — arithmetic, geometry, stereometry, astronomy, and harmony. All of these gradually develop the intellect until at the age of thirty a still smaller number is selected for the study of 'dialectic' or philosophy, which continues for five years.

At the age of thirty-five a man who has passed through this trying course with credit is fit for the highest position in public life, and must, as a public servant, devote his energies to the good of the community till he reaches the age of fifty, when he may retire to devote himself to still further study of philosophy, though he must always be ready to return to the active work of government should the need arise.

The third stage of education is obviously for a small number only; but the second stage concerns all the upper class, i.e., the guardians and rulers.

The most revolutionary feature in the life of the guardians is the communism outlined in the *Republic*. Soldiers must be free from the distractions of family-ties and the necessity of earning their living. All property is therefore to be held in common, and there is community of wives and children. Marriage is strictly regulated by the State, and children are brought up not by their own parents but by specially appointed nurses.[4]

The men and the women — for all duties are shared equally by both sexes — live like soldiers on garrison-duty, and take part in battle side by side. Even the children are to become familiar with war from early childhood. The potter's son learns from watching his father at work, long before he is allowed to touch the wheel, and so the children may learn to fight by watching their parents. As soon as they can learn to ride they are taken out on horseback, under the guidance of some experienced veteran, to watch some military operation from a safe distance. If the battle goes against their side, they are carried away into safety on the first approach of danger.[5]

3

THIS system is interesting both for what it contains and for what it excludes. One of its striking features is the strict censorship of literature and music, on the ground that many of the poets give us a bad impression both of gods and men, whereas we should always teach that the gods are perfect, and hold up for the imitation of the young only such examples of human conduct as we should desire them to follow. Only such music is to be tolerated as shews a martial spirit, other kinds being thought by the writer to be enervating.

This revolt against the arts by a member of an artistic community is surprising to us, who do not so closely connect aesthetic appreciation with morality. Still less can we accept the

'Blood and Iron' system by which children, in addition to being inured to hardship, are from an early age accustomed to view the horrors of war, lest their characters be too much softened by habituation to peaceful pursuits. It is difficult to understand Plato's motive for this ordinance; a study of the recent history of his own countrymen might have taught him that, though perhaps less disciplined than other states, Athens contained good fighting material, and that, to judge by such affairs as those of Melos and Mitylene, their children required no intensive training in bloodthirstiness. This part of education is, however, specially designed for those who belong to the warrior-class, and is so far consistent with Plato's principle that a man cannot follow more than one trade. These children must learn war, just as the craftsmen's children learn a trade, from watching their parents at work.

But the most interesting feature of all in Plato's theoretical system is the attention which he pays to the education of women. In the elementary stage, and subsequently in musical and gymnastic training, there is to be no distinction on the ground of sex. Boys and girls alike are to be trained to wear armour and to use weapons, though after the age of six they no longer attend the same classes. Women of the warrior class fight side by side with men, and women are eligible for the highest office in the State.[6] There is no parallel to this in ancient history.

It has been noted already that neither in Greece nor in Rome was technical training regarded as part of education; education was concerned with moral and intellectual ideals only, and there is no evidence that the Greeks, who were great mathematicians, applied their mathematical ability to practical purposes, at any rate before the time of Archimedes.

The modern architect must be both an artist and a scientist; before he can complete his plans he must make elaborate calculations of stresses, based on mechanical laws now familiar to all, complicated by the consideration of the strengths of the various materials which he proposes to use. The Greek architects probably relied far more on experience and observation than on mathematical formulae, and in their case the happy combination of experiment and inspiration produced, in such buildings as the Erechtheum at Athens, a perfect balance between strength and graceful lightness; while the Romans, aiming more at permanence than beauty, left an enormous margin of safety which makes the best of their buildings, compared with those of the Greeks, appear massive and clumsy.

4

RELIGIOUS teaching had no special place in school education; religious observance played an important part in public and private life, but Greek religion had no creeds or commandments, recognized no sacred books, and was not connected with any ethical teaching. Orthodoxy, for the Athenian, Spartan, or member of any other City-state, involved a tacit admission of the existence of certain divinities, the performance of occasional sacrifices at home, and participation in the more important public observances. Impiety consisted in a disbelief in the divinity of the gods of the State, or a disrespectful attitude towards their worship. The first charge against Socrates was that he did not believe in the gods in whom the State believed, and Anaxagoras was prosecuted and convicted for the expression of unorthodox views in his philosophy, while Alcibiades incurred the charge of having celebrated a blasphemous parody of the Mysteries. Socrates was further prosecuted for introducing new gods, but this charge, unfounded as it was, must be considered as simply vexatious, since no objection was ordinarily made to the celebration of rites in honour of strange gods. The *Republic* of Plato opens with a reference to a festival of the Thracian goddess Bendis, which apparently had some official sanction.

The only dogma to be taught consisted of the ancient myths of the greater and lesser gods and the demigods, and these myths were numerous and often self-contradictory, so that, in the absence of any authorized canon, a man was free to believe as much or as little as he liked of the traditional tales.

The elements of these beliefs were contained in the earliest literature, that of Homer and Hesiod, who, according to Herodotus, made the genealogies of the gods; and as Homer was studied in every school where literature was taught at all, the Greek child learned incidentally as much as he was required to know of theology. Even at Sparta, where literature was at a discount, some Homer was committed to memory, and the boys were taught to recite hymns in honour of the gods. This can hardly be classed as religious instruction in the modern sense of the words, and the teaching of the myths was from quite early times freely criticized by some of the more serious thinkers, on the ground of their non-moral or even immoral tendency. Thus Xenophanes in the fifth century complained that Homer and Hesiod ascribed to the gods all the actions which are regarded as a reproach and a scandal among men.[7] Pindar definitely rejects a story which throws discredit on one of the gods; he revolts against 'calling one of the blessed a glutton,'[8] and the accepted ideas about the Olympian deities came in for criticism both from Aeschylus, who was orthodox, and from Euripides who was so much the reverse as to be nicknamed 'the godless' (ἄθεος). The spirit of revolt against the acceptance of the gross tales of mythology led Metrodorus, a pupil of Anaxagoras, to explain the gods as forces of nature, and both he and Stesimbrotus attempted to explain Homer allegorically. The fact that they did so is an indication of the extraordinary influence of Homer on Greek life. The Homeric poems were regarded with the peculiar reverence which in other countries has generally been reserved for books believed to be divinely inspired. They were supposed to contain useful lessons not only in religion and morality but in all practical affairs. This opinion is pushed to the extreme point of exaggeration in Plato's *Ion,* where the rhapsode of that name maintains that Homer wrote as an expert on all the arts, and consequently he himself, from studying Homer, could take up any profession, even that of a general, though he admits that he is quite lacking in practical experience of military matters.[9]

5

We have referred already to Plato's curious attitude towards the works of the poets — an attitude the more remarkable when we consider how deeply he himself was influenced, as all his contemporaries were, by Homer and the dramatists. He is forced to admit his admiration and appreciation of poetry, but feels on the whole that its moral influence is more often bad than good. Therefore on moral grounds he would banish poetry, if not from the State altogether, at least from its place in the education of children. Certain kinds of literature may have a demoralizing effect on any character, and this is particularly the case with the traditional tales of the heroes and gods, from which the children cannot receive any profit and may suffer serious harm.[10] Learning the myths, they will believe that the divine beings whom they are taught to venerate were worse than the ordinary sinners and criminals of everyday life; that, for instance, they threw their fathers into prison and mutilated them; that they were uncontrolled in their passions, and so forth. Again, if they listen to the poets, they must believe not only that God distributes both blessings and curses at random, but that he may be justified in inflicting punishment. But the truth is that God is never the cause of evil, and therefore all stories which lay the blame on him must be tabooed. This will have the result of cutting out from the school-curriculum considerable portions of the works of the great national poets. Not only the scandalous stories about the gods, but many tales of the heroes and great men of old are demoralizing — any, in fact, which represent them in an unheroic light; we must therefore further exclude all such passages as those in which Homer depicts Achilles abandoning himself to grief over the death of Patroclus, or Priam mourning for Hector.

But what can we do to replace such time-honoured legends? Some religious instruction is indispensable as a basis of morality, but the philosopher's god is not the Zeus or Apollo of ordinary mythology. It is obviously, says Plato, the business of the state to invent, for educational purposes, myths which are moral, and substitute them for the stories which it has rejected.[11] Plato fully recognized the importance of having ideal characters to be held up as examples for imitation; but unfortunately Greek literature contained no 'Lives of the Saints,' as indeed, Greek history had produced no saints, and now that Achilles had been found wanting, there was no one to put in his place. The sophist Prodicus, realizing such a want, had composed the fable of the choice of Heracles; Xenophon regarded the character of Agesilaus as almost ideal. In later times neither the 'great-hearted man' of Aristotle nor the wise man of the Stoics was ever more than an abstraction, and human nature craves for something positive and material. Plato, though he recognized the want, suggested no practical means of supplying it.

Perverse as we may think him in this matter, Plato was at least consistent, in that he would have subjected all imitative arts to a strict censorship: "Must we not," he asks, "control our other artists (in addition to the poets) and prevent them from representing what is vicious, intemperate, mean and indecent in their sculptures and buildings and other products of their art? . . . We do not want our guardians to grow up among images of baseness, as in some rank pasture browsing on noxious herbs and flowers day by day. . . We must rather look for artists who have the gift of catching the nature of beauty and grace, so that our young people may dwell in a land of health, getting the good of all the fair sights and sounds which appeal to their senses like a health-giving breeze that blows from a pure region." [12]

B. XENOPHON [*ca.* 430–*ca.* 354 B.C.]

6

XENOPHON, who is best known as a captain of mercenaries who led the Ten Thousand Greeks on their famous retreat after the battle of Cunaxa, was a friend and pupil of Socrates, who inspired in him an interest in education.

On retiring, in middle life, from his successful career as a soldier of fortune, he settled down on an estate at Scillus, near Olympia, and there, for over twenty years, he divided his time between the occupations of a country-gentleman and literary work. His main preoccupation was history; in addition to the famous *Anabasis* he wrote the *Hellenica,* a history of Greece designed to continue and supplement that of Thucydides. Another important work is the *Memorabilia,* containing reports of numerous conversations between Socrates and various interlocutors. His treatise *On the Lacedaemonian Constitution* contains a sketch of the Spartan educational system on which we have drawn for many details in Chapter I. But the most important source for his views on education in general is the *Cyropaedia,* or Education of Cyrus, which is a kind of historical novel, designed for the edification of the young, and consisting of episodes almost entirely fictitious. Purporting to deal with the life of Cyrus the Great, it begins with an account of Persian education, which is simply an exposition of Xenophon's ideals. A general idea of the scheme may be obtained from a few extracts: "Most governments leave the individual to educate his children as he pleases, and allow the adults to live as they please; and then command them not to steal, not to plunder, not to enter a house by violence, not to strike anyone whom it is not right to strike, not to commit adultery, not to disobey the magistrates, and other things in like manner; and they impose penalties on people who transgress any of these precepts. The Persian laws, on the other hand, by anticipation, provide from the beginning that their citizens shall not be of a character to desire any mean or wicked action. Their method is as follows: they have what is called the Free Agora, where the king's palace and the other official buildings are situated. All things for sale and all traders in these goods, together with their clamour and coarseness, are banished to another place, so that their confusion may not interfere with the orderliness of those who are under instruction. This Agora, round the public buildings, is divided into four quarters. One of these is for boys, one for youths, one for full-grown men, and one for those who are past military age. All of these divisions are obliged by law to attend in their own quarters, the boys and grown men at daybreak, the elders when they find it convenient, except on certain days when their attendance too is compulsory. The youths pass the night in the neighbourhood of the official buildings. . .

The boys attending the public schools spend their time in learning justice, and say that they go there for that purpose, as our boys go to school to learn their letters. . . Boys are also taught self-control, obedience, temperance with regard to eating and drinking. They bring from home bread and cress, and a cup, so that, when thirsty, they may drink water from the river. They learn also to shoot and throw the javelin, and practise these exercises till they are sixteen or seventeen years of age, when they enter the class of Youths." [13]

These ἔφηβοι are for the next ten years occupied with garrison and police duties in the city, where they are assiduously practised in the use of arms. They are constantly taken out, under the superintendence of the king, on long and arduous hunting expeditions, which are a useful preparation for military service. Only at the end of this term are they reckoned as full-grown men.

A comparison of this sketch with parts of

Chapter I will shew how strongly Xenophon was influenced by Spartan ideals.

The second great influence on Xenophon was the example of Socrates. Profoundly impressed by the ethical side of his master's teaching, he regarded right conduct as the end of all education. The most important thing was to train men to see what was right and to act accordingly — to live well and be good citizens. All other things were to him, as an educationist, of minor importance. His description of the Persian schools is quite fictitious, and is drawn chiefly for the purpose of contrasting his own ideals with those of contemporary Athens. The intellectual side is neglected in this imaginary system, just as at Sparta. Men are regarded chiefly with regard to their utility to the State. The Spartan bias again is clear in the importance attached to physical education, and the prominence given to hunting, which was an integral part of Spartan training. The Socratic idea that Conduct is of supreme importance is emphasized throughout; but Socrates, though not a teacher of literature, did not neglect or despise it, but rather took a conventional literary training for granted; thus the system of Xenophon is, by contrast, one-sided and imperfect.

C. ARISTOTLE [384–322 B.C.]

7

THE EDUCATIONAL theories of Aristotle, for many years a pupil and subsequently a critic of Plato, are closely connected with his philosophy. Ethics and Politics were to the Greek mind inseparably connected, and Education is an important branch of the latter science.[14] Aristotle in his *Politics* considers the question whether education should be systematized or not, and decides that it is too important a matter to be left to individual caprice. Education is the only method of instilling 'Virtue.' For the individual there may be some advantages to be obtained from private education, owing to the greater amount of individual attention which is possible, but in general, since it is by education that the State's ends are to be attained, the State must regulate it. It must be uniform and general, since, in the kind of community which he is considering, all in turn may be called upon to take their share in government.[15] Aristotle rejected the Platonic 'communities'; [16] he retained family life, and therefore to some extent home-education. For the rest, he approves on the whole of the ordinary school-subjects, and agrees with Plato's division of education into two main periods, separated by an interval devoted to intensive physical training.

The main difference between Aristotle and his predecessors in theory lies in his greater consideration for the individual. The end of education for each man is to learn how to employ leisure in the best possible way, and the best way is to live the highest life possible for man, which Aristotle eventually finds to lie in *θεωρία*, 'contemplation,' the exercise of the highest functions of the intellect, wherein lies the highest happiness.[17] This is a man's highest duty to himself, so that social efficiency, though extremely important, is not the only, or the highest, human aim.

Aristotle draws a clear distinction between liberal and illiberal elements in education. True education is not concerned with any knowledge which he classifies as *βάναυσος* or 'mechanical.'[18] This class includes handicrafts and wage-earning occupations in general, which he considers likely to drag the mind and body down to a low level, and therefore unworthy of the attention of a free man. Even some liberal arts may, if studied on wrong principles, have a 'banausic' effect. There is nothing new in this attitude; it was the general Greek feeling, for instance, that an amateur must not aim at rivalling a professional in such accomplishments as music.[19] Such prejudices have been known to survive even into modern times.

As to method, Aristotle is really in agreement with Socrates, though his terminology is different. In order to attain virtue we must possess certain inherent qualities, and these must be developed by habituation to what is right. The power of habituation is not unlimited, for, as he says, a stone can never learn to move upwards of itself, however often you try to teach it the habit by throwing it into the air.[20] Given the requisite nature and proper training, a man may attain virtue, but moral virtue at least is only possible in a community; the various virtues cannot be exercized if a man lives alone. Generosity, for instance, requires a receiver as well as a giver.[21] A man must do his best for his fellow-citizens before he can do his best for himself.

He must work in order to prepare himself to use leisure in the best possible way, and the proper use of leisure is not idleness but still higher intellectual effort. For this a liberal education is the only possible means of preparation.[22]

D. ISOCRATES [436–338 B.C.]

8

ISOCRATES was born in the Age of Pericles and lived to see Greek independence overthrown by the victory of Philip of Macedon at Chaeronea. It was in 392 B.C. that, as a man of forty-four, he opened a school of rhetoric at Athens, and in 339 B.C., at the age of ninety-seven, he was still working, with the help of his pupils, at the revision of an earlier composition. He is generally reckoned as one of the great Athenian orators, though he seldom, if ever, spoke in public, being handicapped by a diffident manner and an inadequate voice. He was, therefore, not so much an orator as a teacher of oratory and a writer of oratorical prose, in both of which spheres he was eminent. The majority of his writings are essays put into the form of speeches, of which the political discourses are of supreme value owing to the sagacity and broadmindedness which characterize them. For our purpose the scholastic speeches, dealing with principles of education, are of greater importance.

Isocrates, unlike the Sophists, never lectured to large audiences; he preferred to take not more than two pupils at a time, and to give them individual instruction. The training which he imparted was based on rhetorical composition, but it had a basis much broader than rhetoric, and was characterized by its philosophic outlook, though he was himself no philosopher. What he calls his 'philosophy' is a theory of culture, to be attained by the discipline of discourse (ἡ τῶν λόγων παιδεία), and is, like that of the Sophists, a system of teaching which bears on practical life.[23]

At the beginning of his professional career — about 390 B.C. — Isocrates wrote his earliest work on education, the speech *Against the Sophists*. Only part of the work survives, and this contains only destructive criticism, which was intended to lead up to a statement of the writer's own theory. The loss is to some extent repaired by the constructive statements contained in the speech *On the Antidosis,* published some thirty-five years afterwards.

The introduction to the former speech contains a severe indictment of the general run of professional educators, who promise more than they intend ever to perform. They are divided into three classes. First of all come the professors of 'disputation' or 'eristic,' who promise to impart to their pupils a full knowledge of right conduct, which will lead to perfect happiness. This precious gift they sell for a ridiculously small price. This attack is levelled not at the Sophists whom Plato castigated, but at some of the lesser Socratics, particularly the Megarian school.

The next class to be considered is that of the 'teachers of political discourse,' i.e., practical rhetoric. These, says Isocrates, care nothing for the truth, whereas the 'eristics' at any rate professed to follow it. Their chief object is to attract pupils by specious promises, maintaining that they can teach oratory as easily as the alphabet to anybody who can afford their small fees. Here Isocrates explains his own views, that there are three requisites for success in speech or action — natural ability, theoretical training, and experience. Of these the first is by far the most important, but the teachers in question neglect it.

The third division of the speech is devoted to the compilers of handbooks of rhetoric (τέχναι). These writers profess to aim no higher than the teaching of litigation, a thing offensive in itself. This class of men again is inferior to the 'eristics,' who make a plausible pretence of being concerned with virtue and moderation, while the sole principle of the technical writers is base covetousness.

In the *Antidosis,* Isocrates defends his life and profession. In the first part of the speech he maintains the purity of his aims and the loftiness of his ideals. In the second half he states his theory that 'Philosophy' (i.e., his own system of culture) is for the soul what Gymnastic is for the body. He repeats his earlier statement that, of the three essentials to success, natural aptitude is the most important, though teaching and practice are indispensable. In addition, both teacher and pupil must have determination to persevere, for the necessary training is laborious and must extend over some years. Absolute knowledge of what we ought or ought not to do is unattainable, but the wise man is one who as a general rule can make a satisfactory guess, and a man with a sincere ambition to speak or write well and to persuade others will incidentally improve himself, for character counts for more than anything.

Thus Isocrates, like his contemporaries, deals with practical life, but whereas their aims are mean and narrow, his are broad and enlightened. In particular we must emphasize his efforts to make his pupils look beyond the horizon of the city-state and regard life from a Hellenic point of view. Again, while they were superficial, he was thorough; they preferred short-cuts to learning, while he followed the road, and whereas they would be content with cheap temporary success, he aimed ever at producing results of permanent value.

As a preparation for his own courses he approved of boys learning grammar and poetry, according to custom; later on mathematics and even 'eristic' might be studied as providing good mental training. His own method was to instruct his pupils in all styles of prose-composition — just as the gymnastic master begins by teaching the various thrusts and parries, which are subsequently to be developed into an elaborate system of attack and defence.[24] At the second stage the pupil himself composed exercises on topics carefully chosen with a view to their wide interest, and these were carefully corrected and revised by the master himself. Three or four years, at least, were required for the completion of the course.

E. PLUTARCH [*ca.* 50–120 A.D.]

9

AFTER a long interval we come to Plutarch, who in addition to the famous *Biographies* wrote numerous treatises on ethical subjects, and is concerned with education chiefly from the moral point of view. Deferring for a time the spurious tract *On the education of children* (*vide infra* p. 166), we find certain treatises which bear his name dealing chiefly with adult education. He is concerned solely with the leisured class, and, in the extant works, only with men, though he sometimes admits that women too should be educated, and he is credited with a treatise, *A plea for women's education* (*Mulieres erudiendas esse*), now unfortunately lost.

Education means to him a process begun at birth and continuing till death, and is concerned with all human faculties — the energies of the body, the passions, and the intellect; the ultimate aim being the perfection of the soul. The body is to be carefully trained by proper diet and exercise; the emotions must be regulated; the intellect stimulated by independent thought and concentration. The value of literature is chiefly moral rather than artistic; history has an ethical rather than a practical value; the natural sciences and mathematics prepare the way for the highest study, philosophy, which itself merges into theology and prepares man for the revelation of perfect knowledge in the life after death. Plutarch was himself a great teacher, by his lectures, his conversation, and his writings; but he never formulated a theory of education. He appears to have taken for granted the existence of the ordinary school and university courses of his day. From his extant works, however, especially the moral treatises, we may collect scattered hints of the principles underlying his method. Regarding the Progress towards Virtue [25] as the object of all education, he was much concerned with psychology, especially as applied to the passions and the reason, two elements which are in continual conflict. His tract *De cohibenda ira* contains many precepts on self-control, the point of view being mainly individualistic, for Plutarch considered the effect of the various passions on the man who gives way to them rather than on others. Thus he wishes that a kind friend would hold a mirror up to him when he loses his temper — the sight of his own distorted face would be a deterrent.[26] Himself a man of the widest reading — he is estimated to have quoted from over a hundred and fifty different authors — he gave his pupils the full benefit of his literary knowledge; but his literary criticism is based entirely on ethical principles, reproducing in another form the sort of criticism of poetry which we have found in Plato's Republic.[27] Like the sophist Ion, he regards Homer as the source of history, philosophy, and politics,[28] and even discovers in him the germs of rhetoric, strategy, medicine, and all forms of literature.[29] The use of history is that it gives examples of passions properly or improperly treated.[30] Music too, he thought, should be studied on account of its influence on the emotions, though it also has an intellectual aspect.[31] Here again much of Plato's teaching is reproduced.

Perhaps the most important item, to us, in all his teaching, is the recognition of the necessity of effort on the part of the learner. The pupil must not be a mere receptacle for knowledge poured into him by the teacher; he has a personal responsibility. Pupils should be encouraged to ask questions, but only to a certain point: they must not do so merely to save themselves the trouble of thinking.[32]

Plutarch accepted without question the usual methods of physical exercise, and approved the strenuous training of the Spartans, but this was a subject in which he took no special interest.[33] He devoted, however, a treatise to the care of the body,[34] the keynote of which is moderation. We must avoid excess in eating, especially with regard to meat; wine should be taken, but in moderation. The body should not be neglected for the mind, any more than the mind should be starved at the expense of the body; both should be exercised together.[35]

Though Plutarch lived at a time (*vide infra* Chapter VI), when the education of the whole civilized world was built on a rhetorical foundation, and though he himself was a trained rhetorician, he neglected rhetoric except as a special study for practical statesmen; his own system was not directed to practical ends, and was thus notably out of keeping with the spirit of his times.

IV. ROME

I

GREECE, from the earliest historical times, had the best foundation for a literary education, namely a remarkable literature. The poems of Homer preceded the rise and organization of the city-states of European Greece and Asia Minor; the work of Hesiod was, so far as we know, given to the world before those states had advanced far enough in material prosperity to have leisure for the pursuit of culture. The lyric poets were the product of some of those cities themselves in their early days.

The absence of literary study from early Roman education is sufficiently explained by the fact that no national literature existed. Rome had no Homer to inspire her; for the first five centuries after the foundation of the city she was occupied in fighting for existence, for independence, and finally for dominion. No time was left for any but the military arts, the intervals between the periods of fighting being mostly devoted to agriculture by that *rusticorum mascula militum proles,* whom Horace extols.[1] Down to the latter half of the third century B.C. verse composition was represented only by a few rude ballads and ritual hymns, while prose — even if we give the term its widest signification, namely that which is not verse — consisted only of laws, treaties, and commemorative inscriptions. The capture of Tarentum in 272 B.C. brought the Romans into contact with a civilization which both in its material and intellectual aspects was higher than their own; the annexation of Sicily in 241 B.C. strengthened the contact, and during the generation which followed the first Punic War the Romans at last, after centuries of fighting, found leisure for studying the arts of peace. A humanistic movement began, and soon involved many of the more serious-minded men of high position who had won renown as soldiers and statesmen. From this epoch we date the beginning of Roman literature. After the capture of Tarentum, Andronicus, a Greek prisoner of war, passed as a slave into the hands of one Livius, and was employed as tutor to give instruction to the children of his master and others who visited the house.

Eventually obtaining his freedom he took his former master's name, and was known as Lucius Livius Andronicus. He continued to live at Rome as the first schoolmaster, or rather private tutor, who followed Greek methods, and for the use of his pupils he translated Homer's *Odyssey* into Latin verse, using the old Saturnian metre. He also wrote poems of his own in the Latin language. A generation later Ennius (239–169 B.C.), the real father of Roman poetry, broadened and secured the foundations of a national literature.

2

CICERO in his treatise *De Republica*,[2] a work which survives only in a fragmentary state, made Scipio, the chief character in the dialogue, contrast Greek and Roman principles of education, remarking that Roman institutions were opposed to any system of compulsory education. In this he was no doubt thinking of Spartan, rather than Athenian, practice. Our knowledge of Roman education in early times is somewhat scanty, but the system, such as it was, must be regarded as closely bound up with the thoroughly Roman institution of *patria potestas*, by which the head of a household had, according to law, absolute right of control over his children, a control so thorough that he could, at least in theory, sell them into slavery or kill them if he chose.

Thus it might be held that any father had a perfect right to neglect his children and allow them to grow up quite illiterate; but public opinion on the one hand, and on the other that strong sense of duty and patriotism which characterized the citizens of the early Republic, made such neglect impossible. The *pater-familias* had his duties towards every member of his household as well as his rights over them; and though the rights were not fully exercised, the duties were never forgotten. The boy would spend his first few years under the care of his mother, or of some female relation, who superintended both his simple lessons and his games; but before childhood was past, the father normally took entire charge of the son's upbringing. Down to the latter half of the third century B.C. the boy, if we may trust the authorities, who, it is true, are somewhat late, had his father for his only schoolmaster.[3] From him he learned to read and write, to run and to swim; he worked with him on the farm, attended him while he performed the domestic sacrifices, accompanied him when he visited the houses of friends, and helped to serve the guests at table. He was taken sometimes to the forum to listen to the public speeches, and might even, if his father was a senator, be admitted to a place near the door in the Senate-house, there to become familiar at an early age with the formalities of the house's procedure.[4] This close parental association was, in early times, continued till the boy assumed the *toga virilis,* at the age of sixteen.

At a later period we find a development of the same educational principle in the *tirocinium fori,* a kind of informal apprenticeship by which a boy on the verge of manhood was put under the charge of some distinguished public man from whose example he might learn oratory and the principles of statesmanship. Cicero relates how he himself was taken by his father to the famous jurist Mucius Scaevola, and ordered, as far as possible, never to leave his side.[5]

The content of this early education was scanty: reading and writing were, of course, included, and arithmetic of a simple nature, sufficient, at any rate, for the keeping of farm-accounts. The literary and artistic sides were normally neglected; there was little or no literature in early days to be studied, but boys were instructed in the legends of their country which passed for history, preserved, probably, in verse-form in the rude Saturnian metre. These they learned to recite or sing, and they were also required to make themselves familiar with the content of the laws, at any rate from the time when law was codified in the XII Tables. This custom persisted long after the old system had been modified by Greek ideas, for Cicero remarks that in his childhood all boys thus learned the laws by heart. By the time of his manhood the practice had been dropped, since the old laws had been to a great extent superseded by the praetor's edict.[6]

Although a great variety of dialects, and several languages, including Greek, were current in Italy before it became Romanized, and for purposes of intercourse a knowledge of these must have been useful if not essential, there is no evidence of any language other than Latin having been taught in a school during this early period. The fine arts were in general neglected, but this neglect cannot have been so universal as is sometimes imagined, for

Gaius Fabius Pictor, the grandfather of the historian of the same name, received his title from having painted frescoes in the temple of Salus (302 B.C.), which were still admired in the Augustan age; and the Capitoline Wolf (296 B.C.) proves that in metal casting the Roman craftsmen were the equals of any of their contemporaries.[7] With such crafts, however, the general course of education was not concerned.

3

At what period elementary schools were instituted at Rome it is hard to determine, since the evidence is conflicting and unsatisfactory. Plutarch asserts that the first school was opened by one Spurius Carvilius, a freedman who lived about the middle of the third century B.C.,[8] but the national legends contain many references to school-life at a much earlier date; even Romulus and Remus are said to have attended a school at Gabii,[9] and Virginia was seized and carried off on her way to school by the freedmen of Appius Claudius the decemvir. Livy in recounting the story definitely states that the grammar schools (*litterarum ludi*) were situated in booths (*tabernae*) in the forum.[10] Attempts have been made to reconcile the statements of Livy and Plutarch by assuming that Carvilius was the first schoolmaster to receive definite fees, while his predecessors had been content with voluntary gifts from the parents, like the advocates, who though not permitted to charge fees to their clients, nevertheless made a good business out of their pleading.

We must assume that these early schools, at whatever date instituted, merely supplied the education which was normally given by the father in cases when, for various reasons, the parents were unable to undertake their children's instruction.

4

THE BROADENING of outlook brought about by the first contact with Greek civilization, mentioned above (p. 92), began to react on Roman education in the middle of the third century B.C. The result was a complete change of principle, and the development on a literary foundation of a system which was to last for about a hundred and fifty years.

We have seen that Livius was the first professional teacher on Greek lines. The poet

Ennius himself eked out the rather scanty emoluments obtainable by the translation of plays for the stage by teaching Greek to some members of the noble families,[11] but was not, so far as we know, concerned with a school of any kind. We hear, however, that he was the author of books on grammar, spelling, pronunciation, and metre, and to him are ascribed four volumes of translations from Greek authors, an indication that there already existed in Rome a reading public, to satisfy whose demand this supply was provided. Shortly after his death the Greek Crates of Mallos gave lectures on literary subjects in Rome. It must not be assumed that the old practical education was at once entirely superseded, but there was a growing tendency to modify and to supplement it by the literary culture adopted from Greece.[12]

5

THIS humanistic movement was from the first fostered by a number of men in high position, such as Scipio Africanus, but many Romans of the old school still looked with grave suspicion on the introduction of the humane studies into education. At a time when private life at Rome was thus undergoing a rapid change, Cato the Censor (234–149 B.C.) is a typical survivor of the old school of thought, suspicious of all innovation and profoundly distrustful of everything foreign. Plutarch thus describes the way in which he took sole charge of his son's education:

"As soon as ever his son was born, however urgent the business upon his hands, unless it related to public affairs, he would be by when his wife swaddled and washed the child. When the boy began to understand, Cato himself took charge and began to teach him his letters, though he had a cultured slave called Chilon who was actually a schoolmaster and taught several other children. As he himself said, he did not care for his son to be rebuked by a slave or have his ears pulled because he was slow at his lessons; but he was himself the schoolmaster, the teacher of law, and the gymnastic instructor, and taught his son to box, to endure heat and cold, and to swim the rough waters of the swirling river. He tells us that he even wrote a history for him with his own hand in big letters, so that the boy might profit at home by experience of his ancestors' virtues. He was as careful to avoid any use of improper language in his son's presence as in the presence of the Vestal Virgins."[13]

It was particularly against the invasion of Greek ideas that Cato sustained throughout the greater part of his life a losing battle, fighting for the old education as Cato the younger fought for the old régime.[14] In the end he confessed himself beaten, and he is said to have learned Greek in his old age; but we may note throughout his writings examples of his strong conservatism.[15] Thus, "It is," he says, "worth while to glance at Greek literature, but not to make a close study of it (*inspicere, non perdiscere*)." "Believe me," he writes, "my words are prophetic: when that race gives us its literature, it will corrupt everything."[16] The old Roman was as suspicious of Greek science as he was of Greek letters. He goes on to tell his son to beware of Greek physicians, for "they have bound themselves by a curse to kill all barbarians by their medicine." "But they will take fees for doing it; realizing that men value more what they have to pay for, they will set up as regular practitioners, and, thus obtaining our confidence, have every opportunity of destroying us."[17] He himself had compiled a book of simples, interspersed with certain charms and incantations in whose efficacy he thoroughly believed.[18]

Literary culture he considered unnecessary; the chief qualifications by which a man could become a good citizen were a knowledge of law, agriculture and war, practice in public speaking, and medicine of the primitive kind which he himself practised.

Though oratory was of primary importance to Cato for the training of a statesman, he was fundamentally opposed to the rhetorical artifice of the Greek schools. His own principles are embodied in his apophthegm: *Rem tene, verba sequentur*—"Keep to the point, and the words will come of themselves."[19] It was this keeping to the point which was the secret of his success in the innumerable cases in which he was a pleader, for his obstinate persistence wore out all opposition. In spite of his influence, Greek rhetoric was during this period extensively studied at Rome. Some attempt was made also to introduce music and dancing, but proficiency in these arts, even down to a much later period, was looked upon with suspicion as being foreign to the Roman character.

But if Cato represents one side of opinion at Rome, we may take Aemilius Paulus as typical of the other.[20] The conqueror of Perseus of Macedon himself brought up his two sons, Fabius and Scipio Aemilianus, according to the old Roman tradition, but, having an exceptional zeal for Greek learning, he obtained for them Greek instructors in grammar, logic and rhetoric, drawing, and other subjects. He had already brought to Rome a collection of Greek books to form a library in his own house, and is said to have invited the Athenians to send a philosopher to conduct his sons' higher education. When, in 167 B.C., the historian Polybius came to Italy as one of a thousand hostages demanded from Achaea, he was fortunate in being welcomed by the sons of Paulus. Scipio, the younger son, who was then eighteen years of age, conceived a warm affection for the exile, which lasted throughout life, to the great advantage of both. Scipio, called at an early age to the responsibility of high military command, took Polybius with him on all his campaigns, and profited by the advice of his companion, who was not only a sound theorist but a man of wide practical experience. Polybius, thus taken to the bosom of the exclusive military aristocracy, had exceptional opportunities of obtaining material for his great history, to the composition of which he devoted the latter half of his life.[21]

6

FROM about 100 B.C. onwards, roughly, for two centuries, we find Roman education running closely on Greek lines. Even in early childhood Greek influence was felt, at any rate among the upper classes, for whose children Greek nurses were commonly employed. The boy from the age of seven to the age of sixteen was, like the boy in fifth century Athens, put under the charge of a paedagogus, who escorted him to school, attended him constantly, and incidentally gave him lessons in Greek. Sometimes also he was attended by a slave who carried his books and a lantern, for he might in winter have either to go or return in darkness; and the streets of Rome were rough and not lighted at all, and evil characters prowled about after dark. The dangers of the streets are vividly described at a later age by Juvenal,[22] and conditions were probably no better under the Republic than in the time of the Emperors. During the last century of the pagan era we have definite reference to social distinctions in schools, at any rate as between the country towns and the capital city. Horace gives us some valuable hints in connection with the story of his own childhood.[23] His father was unwilling to send him to school in his native town, to mix with the sons of burly centurions who went there with their satchels and slates slung over their shoulders, for the poorer classes could not afford a paedagogus, and further, perhaps, in a country-place such supervision was unnecessary. The good man decided to take his son to Rome and give him as good an education as any knight or senator could obtain for his son. No doubt Horace's father attached importance to the social atmosphere of the better-class school, but what Horace is particularly grateful for is the sound education which he received.

7

THE ELEMENTARY school was, with unconscious irony, called *ludus* (play). Schools of more advanced instruction came to be known, with equal inappropriateness, as *scholae* from the Greek σχολή, which originally meant leisure.

The boys rose very early; Juvenal's reference to lessons beginning soon after midnight is no doubt an absurd exaggeration; but many passages in literature establish the fact that early rising was a habit with Romans of all classes,[24] and it may be accepted that they started off some time before daybreak. If they had not time for breakfast at home, they had an opportunity to buy rolls from the baker on their way to school.[25] They returned home for the midday meal, and then went back again to school. Early school was for them, as for boys of all times, an unpopular institution, and the only light was from the evil-smelling and smoky lamps which all the pupils took with them.

No special kind of building was required for a school; we commonly hear of lessons being given in a *pergula*, which may mean either a kind of ground-floor verandah, roofed, but open at the sides, or possibly something like the open-fronted shops which may be seen at Pompeii.[26] We suppose, then, that a school was normally a ground-floor room open to the air on at least one side. The head teacher sat on a chair (*cathedra*), sometimes on a raised daïs (*pulpitum*); his assistant, if there was one, had a stool, while the pupils had benches. There were probably no tables or desks, but the children rested their books and writing tablets on their knees. Some schoolrooms were furnished with busts of famous authors,[27] and the walls were decorated with tablets representing well-known scenes of history and mythology. Several such drawings have been preserved, though often in a very fragmentary state. The most famous is the one now in the Capitoline Museum, the *Tabula Iliaca* representing scenes from the Trojan War.[28] There is no evidence that maps were used in school-teaching, or that geography was studied at school,[29] though maps were not unknown.

The schoolmaster (*ludi magister*) taught, first, reading and writing. The first reading lessons were sometimes treated more or less as a game. Horace refers to the teachers giving little cakes as prizes to children learning their letters,[30] while Quintilian refers with approval to the practice current in his time of giving them ivory letters to play with, and recommends the use of any device which may promote an interest in lessons.[31] For writing, wax tablets were used on which letters were written for the child to copy (*praescriptum*), the teacher in early stages guiding the inexpert pupil's hand. Quintilian also recommends the use of letters incised on a tablet; the pupil will acquire dexterity by following the lines with his stilus, which the deep grooves will keep in its place, so that the child will feel that he is doing something by himself without the teacher's aid.[32] Simple arithmetic was taught by counting on the fingers or with the *abacus*, that is, a calculating board.

Corporal punishment was frequent, and the typical schoolmaster is commonly referred to as a noisy bully; Horace's master, Orbilius, had a bad reputation for frequent use of the cane,[33] and Martial, who lived near an elementary school, complained that the noise of shouts and floggings kept him awake in the early morning.[34] Quintilian, with a humanity beyond the common run of his contemporaries, deprecated the excessive use of physical punishment.[35]

About the number and duration of holidays there is some doubt. Certainly the schools were closed on the occasions of the Saturnalia which originally occupied one day only but were later extended to three and eventually to seven days, and of the Quinquatrus, the five days' festival of Minerva in March.[36] Presumably lessons must have stopped also on other days of general holiday, for instance, for the Circus Games. It is estimated that the most important fixed festivals, seven in number, occupied sixty-two days in all, minor celebrations and occasional shows of gladiators might account for a few more in the course of the year, and we have at least one hint of the possibility of half holidays on market-days, which occurred on every eighth day. "The boys look forward to the market-days," says Varro, "so that the master may let them out to play."[37]

Certainly some schools enjoyed a long summer holiday. An often-quoted line of Horace, referring to the country school in his native town, is generally taken to mean that fees were paid only during eight months of the year, i.e., the holidays lasted for four months; and this is supported by Martial, who, writing in July, says that the cane is to have a rest till the Ides of October; for if boys can keep their health in the summer, that is all the learning they need.[38] On the other hand, Ovid, in an address to schoolmasters at the Quinquatrus, observes that "the goddess now brings them new pupils," implying obviously that the school-year begins after this festival, and Macrobius makes it clear that in his time an annual payment for tuition was made in March, as opposed to the monthly fees mentioned by Horace.[39] Possibly the arrangements for the higher schools were different from those prevailing in the elementary ones.

8

THE GREAT majority of Roman children never got beyond this elementary education. The boys of the poorer classes would leave school as soon as they were old enough to help their fathers in the family trade or business; the girls went to help their mothers at home, and early marriages were common, twelve being the legal age. But the sons of the privileged classes, or of any who could afford it, passed from the *ludus* to the care of the *grammaticus,* in a separate school, where they were introduced to the study of literature. In the early days of Graeco-Roman education Homer was one of the regular set books, but at a later time Roman literature was also used. Horace refers to having received lessons in Homer at Rome, and also to having the poems of Livius dictated to him.[40] Virgil and Cicero became school-classics, and Horace prophesies for his book of *Epistles* a dreadful fate — that in old age it may be used in remote country-schools to teach children the alphabet.[41]

The teachers were for the most part either Greeks or men trained under Greek methods, and at this point we meet a fundamental difference between Greek and Roman education. The Greeks, even the Athenians, who were probably the best educated and most liberal minded with regard to culture, at any rate in the Golden Age of Greece, paid no attention to foreign languages or literature. Themistocles, who had dealings with Persia all his life, did not begin to study the Persian language till the time of his exile, towards the end of his career.[42] The national literature was the only one that was ever studied either in the schools or outside. But in Rome as early as the second century B.C. a foreign ambassador could address the senate in the Greek language without the need of an interpreter, and during the period with which we are now dealing, Greek language and literature were regular subjects for school-study; so much so, that it was a matter of debate among theorists whether Greek or Latin should be studied first.[43] Thus the Romans had declared definitely in favour of the principle which has pervaded education ever since, that some attention at least should be paid to the comprehension of ideas expressed in an alien language. This striking innovation, due rather to the accident of circumstances than to design, puts all subsequent ages under a debt to Rome. Homer was, at any rate in some schools, the first poet to be studied. Here the Romans were following without question the practice which the Greeks had deliberately adopted of introducing pupils at an early age to the greatest masterpieces of literature. What custom had sanctioned, Quintilian, the greatest of Roman theorists, approved. His opinion is that boys will be insensibly influenced by a study of what is great, even though they cannot at first fully appreciate the greatness.[44] Virgil's work came to the front very soon after the poet's death, and has ever since occupied a unique position in school-curricula.[45] Cicero approves of the study of Hesiod by the son of his friend Lepta; Ovid mentions the comedies of Menander as being read by boys and girls alike. We know from Horace that the old Roman poets were studied at school. Of the Greek tragedians there is little mention, though later on we find Augustine objecting to their use in schools on moral grounds.[46] The Alexandrine poets, though widely read in literary circles, were evidently reserved for a later stage of education. In general the choice of books was left to the teacher's taste.

A prominent place was given to *recitatio*, or reading aloud. The pupils would read a passage, being taught to give special attention to proper pronunciation and intonation; they then listened to detailed comments by the master. They also learned poetry by heart, but not to so great an extent as the Greek boys in the classical period, when it was not an unheard-of feat to be able to recite the whole of the *Iliad* or *Odyssey*. Sometimes they were made to write out, as a first exercise in composition, and in simple language, the substance of some story; for instance, a fable of Aesop, which had been recently read; or they might be called upon to paraphrase in prose a piece of poetry which they had studied.[47] Translation from Greek into Latin was practised, but rather as a linguistic exercise than with a view to the formation of literary style.

In general, as it would seem to us, too much was left for the teacher to do; the learning was mostly passive and receptive. Instruction was chiefly in the form of lectures, of which the pupils had to take notes. A great deal was expected of the master; in dealing with a text (*enarratio*) he would explain all the incidents described by the author; he must be familiar with all the allusions and be able to adduce from other sources parallel passages to illustrate the matter in hand; he must have mythology and history at his finger-tips; the life of the author, the circumstances under which he wrote, and the purpose of his poem would naturally find a place in the exposition.[48] The sort of question to which he might be expected to have an answer ready was 'Who was Hecuba's mother?' or 'What song did the Sirens sing?'—a conundrum actually propounded by Tiberius[49] to a schoolmaster; while many others similarly futile are recorded by classical writers.

Further, he would criticize the style—Virgil himself, we know, did not escape castigation at the hands of the grammar-teachers—and would use a passage of the author as a text for a lesson in grammar. He must know at least a little about music, with which the comprehension of rhythm and metre is intimately linked; of astronomy, since the seasons are marked by the rising and setting of the constellations; of philosophy, in order to elucidate Empedocles or Lucretius, who embodied philosophy in their poetry.[50] He must himself possess a certain gift of eloquence to make his teaching impressive.

Grammar was a subject which seems to have had a particular appeal to the Roman mind. The learning of declensions and conjugations was a matter for the elementary school; but at a higher stage a study was made of the parts of speech and their uses, and some attention was paid to what we should call historical grammar and elementary philology.

The work done at school often overlapped that which normally belonged to the rhetorical schools, intended for older pupils, and it is difficult to say how far prose-composition was actually pursued under normal school conditions. Verse-composition must have been frequently studied, at any rate by the clever boys; we have no actual reference to its place in a school-course, but we know that Cicero was quite young when he translated the poems of

Aratus into quite respectable Latin hexameters; Virgil composed the *Culex* at sixteen; Persius had already produced poems at a similar age. The younger Pliny wrote a Greek tragedy — at least, he says, "it was called a tragedy" — at the age of fourteen.[51] Nero had a taste for verse-writing in childhood. Finally there is extant an inscription in honour of a boy who, dying before the age of twelve, had won a prize for Greek verse given by Domitian in 94 A.D.[52] We know definitely that the 'grammar' school instruction comprised, as we have seen above, the laws of metre, and it is natural to suppose that exercises on these rules, in the form of original composition, were not uncommon.

Thus the content of education had now entirely changed. Of the subjects which Cato regarded as the only necessary accomplishments — agriculture, law, war, medicine, and oratory — the first three had passed into the province of specialists. Varro (116–27 B.C.), though himself an agricultural scientist, did not regard agriculture as part of a general education; the arts which he discussed were grammar, dialectic, and rhetoric, followed by geometry, arithmetic, astronomy, music, medicine, and architecture. Of these the first three are identical with the *trivium*, or elementary course, and the next four with the *quadrivium*, or advanced course — the two groups which, taken in connection, formed the basis of education throughout the Middle Ages.

9

As IN modern times the work of the highest classes in school overlaps to some extent the work of Universities, so in the Roman system the work of the grammarian's school encroached to some extent on the higher studies of the rhetorical course. We have seen that the school-exercises included the writing of paraphrases, the reproduction of stories, and, to some extent, original composition of the nature of essay-writing; the preliminary training in the rhetorical schools contained the same *progymnasmata*.[53] A subject was set on which a narrative was first written, derived either from fable or history. Next came the critical treatment of narratives, i.e., arguments either for or against the truth of the story; then came panegyrics or invectives. Another somewhat similar exercise was to take a well-known saying, paraphrase it so as to bring out the meaning, then to argue for the validity of the statement, to draw examples from history, etc. The essay was rounded off with a conclusion which pointed the moral.[54]

All this is preparatory to the serious work of the rhetorician, which begins at this point with the composition of 'declamations.' The details of the instruction recommended by writers of treatises on rhetoric may be passed over, as belonging rather to a technical study of the history of rhetoric than to a general view of education. Apart, however, from theories, we know that declamation, both in Greek and in Latin, was regularly practised by aspirants to success in the courts. Cicero never allowed his faculties to rust in this respect, and, in addition to declaiming, he, and others of his age, composed essays on general topics, particularly on the so-called *communes loci,* or commonplaces, which were bound to occur at some time or other for consideration in actual cases. Here they were following in life the methods learnt in the schools.[55]

By the time of Quintilian the theorists recognized two kinds of declamations: the *suasoria* and the *controversia.* In the purpose of either it was the custom to take some case, either imaginary or from real life; then in the *suasoria* some course of action was recommended, in the *controversia* some proposition was discussed. Juvenal, in describing his early training, says: "I too in my time have advised Sulla to retire into private life and sleep soundly" — evidently referring to a stock subject of a *suasoria*.[56] The elder Seneca made in the time of Tiberius a collection of such essays, containing one book of *suasoriae* and ten of *controversiae,* all taken from the 'fair copies' written by eminent rhetoricians of the time. The following are examples of the subjects: Alexander deliberates whether he shall cross the Ocean; The Spartans debate whether they shall flee from Xerxes; Agamemnon considers the necessity of sacrificing his daughter Iphigenia — these are all *suasoriae:* the *controversiae* were taken from imaginary scenes in history, or from romantic tales, of which the following are representative: Popillius was successfully defended by Cicero on a charge of parricide. When the latter was proscribed, Popillius was sent to kill him, and did so. He is now accused *de moribus*. Again: A man captured by pirates escapes by the help of the leader's daughter, whom he promises to marry.

His father orders him to divorce her and marry an heiress; on his refusal, the father disinherits him. Judging from these examples we conclude that old and trite themes were preferred: many, for instance, were taken not even from quasi-history, but from mythology, and that, Greek. Thus the cases discussed came to be further and further removed from reality, and in the end very little attention is paid to the substance of the speech; it is the form of presentation, the style and the language that count. The practice and principles of the rhetors are thus diametrically opposed to those of old Cato, whose maxim *rem tene, verba sequentur* has been quoted in an earlier chapter. Incidentally the practice of the rhetors exercised a baneful influence on the national literature. It has been a commonplace since the time of Quintilian to call Lucan more of a rhetorician than a poet; but much earlier writers suffered from the Roman tendency to place sound before sense; even the great Virgil is not free from the contagion. Messalla, one of the characters in Tacitus' dialogue *de Oratoribus,* complains that education is deteriorating because pupils become addicted prematurely to the tricks of the rhetorical trade;

they have no time to acquire the 'humanity,' based on history and philosophy and other liberal studies, which Cicero thought indispensable to the true orator. This recalls the attitude of serious Greek thinkers, such as Plato and Socrates, towards the sophists called the 'eristics,' whose sole aim was the attainment of skill in controversy.

10

IN THE early days of Rome the boy learned at home his whole duty to his family and his whole duty to the State; in the same way he learned his duty to the gods. In the course of time the home-education in secular matters was first supplemented and at last practically superseded by school-education; but religious instruction never became a subject for the schools. The early religion of Italy did not involve any body of doctrines or ethical principles, but consisted of a code of observances. Some dues must be paid, certain things must not be done, if the support of the unseen powers was to be secured and their displeasure avoided. Thus traditional piety consisted of observances. Every household made daily offerings to Vesta, the goddess of the hearth, to the Penates, who presided, originally, over the larder, and to the Lares, whose chief interest was the family estate. Prayer and sacrifice to appropriate deities were regularly offered before any seasonal work connected with the farm could be safely begun. Ceres, Mars, and a host of known and even unknown powers, of greater or less importance, must be propitiated on various occasions. The oldest literary composition in the Latin language is the song of the Arval brothers, addressed to the Lares and Marmar, the gods who granted increase to crops and cattle.

In quite early times, however, about 500 B.C., Rome began to add to this primitive nature-worship the worship of the great deities of Olympus, who were supposed to exist in bodily form, and whose divinity was located in temples. The cult of all of the gods was regarded as essential to the welfare of the State, and its importance is proved by the great efforts made by Augustus to restore it to its lost prominence.[57] But this again was more a question of ritual than of religious feeling; the speculations of philosophers as to the nature of God and the possibility of an after-life became, under Greek influence, matters of great interest to the learned classes, providing them with inspiration, and, especially in the darkest days of the early Empire, with spiritual consolation; but they cannot be supposed to have influenced the whole people strongly.

Children from their earliest days became familiar with the ritual of the home and the farm; in later years participation in the greater ceremonial of public propitiation or thanksgiving made them familiar with the details of the State-religion; but it is probable that to the individual it was the home-worship that was more important. There is much significance in the old legend that Terminus, the god who presided over boundaries, refused to abandon his place even to Jupiter himself. Thus religion was closely bound up with the other duties imposed by tradition on every well-brought-up Roman — the custom of his ancestors (*mos maiorum*). Questions of morality, public and private, were generally considered as things largely apart from religious sanction. The schools were no more concerned with a boy's duty to the gods than they were with his duty to his parents; it was taken for granted that he knew both before he went to school.

V. ROMAN THEORY

A. CICERO [106–43 B.C.]

I

WE HAVE seen something of Roman education as it was; it remains for us to consider the theories of the chief contemporary writers on the subject, and to see how far practice and theory agreed. The most important theorists are Cicero and Quintilian, of whom the former was born in 106 B.C., while the latter died *ca.* 100 A.D., so that their lives cover some two thirds of the period during which Roman education attained its fullest development.

Cicero was the ablest and most successful advocate of his day; though not successful as a statesman he was a man who counted in politics; his knowledge of Greek philosophy surpassed that of any of his contemporaries, and though not himself an original philosopher he had a great gift for popular exposition of the subject. The ideal of Roman citizenship which he always held before himself was the good orator. He took as the foundation of such a character Cato's definition of an orator, 'A good man skilled in speaking' (*Vir bonus dicendi peritus*), but his requirements were far in excess of Cato's.[1] The one, as we know, thought little of literary accomplishments, and emphasized chiefly the importance of moral worth and skill in certain practical subjects; Cicero considered that the widest education was necessary to the orator. His theories of education are to be found chiefly in certain dialogues, of which the *de Oratore* is the most important. The three books of this treatise, composed when his intellectual powers were at their height and his style had reached perfect maturity, are really an essay, or rather a series of essays, on the power of oratory and the accomplishments which the orator needs to equip him for his task; but it is cast in the form of a dialogue, in supposed imitation of Plato, though the long continuous discourses of which it consists resemble more the lectures of the Sophists than the discussion based on questions and answers which is the essence of the Platonic style. The chief characters in the dialogue are L. Licinius Crassus, the most illustrious orator before the time of Cicero; M. Antonius, the grandfather of the triumvir, whom some critics placed on a level with Crassus as an orator; P. Sulpicius Rufus, a brilliant speaker who perhaps relied more on natural gifts than on training; and C. Aurelius Cotta, whose *forte* was the careful arrangement of argument. Minor parts are played by Q. Mucius Scaevola, the augur, Q. Lutatius Catulus, once the colleague of Marius in the consulship, and C. Julius Caesar Strabo Vopiscus, a son of Catulus' mother by a second husband. All of these were eminent for their oratory, though in somewhat different styles, with the exception of Scaevola, who, as an expert jurist, somewhat questions the high value assigned to rhetoric.

Cicero divides instruction into two grades, the former of which he calls *puerilis institutio*, the second being an advanced course which will result in the acquirement of a *politior humanitas*.[2] This word, which Cicero was the first to apply to general culture, has played, and still plays a great part in the history of education; 'humanistic' is the term applied to the learning of the Renaissance; and at the present day the Final School of Classical Honours at Oxford is known as *Litterae humaniores*.

On the education of children he did not write; we know that his own son was educated at home with the son of his brother Quintus; competent tutors were employed, and though Cicero kept an eye on their progress he had not time to teach them personally. They were brought up much in the same way as the sons of Aemilius Paulus in an earlier age. When they had made some progress with rhetoric, he decided to give them some instruction himself.[3]

He expresses definite opinions about the more advanced education given in the School of the *grammaticus* as opposed to the *puerilis institutio* under the *ludi magister* or *litterator* (see above pp. 105 ff.). In the preface to the *de Oratore* he names the 'arts' taught in the schools of his day — philosophy, mathematics, music, literature, and rhetoric; and later in the same work[4] geometry and astronomy are added to the mathematical studies, so that we have from Cicero a list of seven 'arts' to which he was the first to apply the term *liberal arts* which became the commonplace of the Middle Ages. Other writers of his time and a little later give somewhat different lists, but there is a permanent substratum of literature and mathematics.[5]

2

THE DUTIES of the *grammaticus* are defined as follows by Cicero, speaking in the person of Crassus, a character in the dialogue: "to comment on the poets, to teach history, to explain the meaning of words, to impart a correct accent and delivery."[6] It is remarkable that history was not mentioned among the liberal arts, for it was a subject to which Cicero attached great importance. He does not discuss the question what authors should be studied, nor in what language lessons should be given; but the tutors whom he employed for his son were all Greeks, so that the presumption is that the Latin language was kept in the background.[7] Some years later, writing to his son at Athens, he advises the young man not to neglect his native language.[8] He himself, as the frequent quotations in his dialogues and even in some speeches shew, was exceptionally well read in the old Roman poets.

We have seen (p. 117) that school-work sometimes encroached on rhetorical studies, and

Cicero evidently approved of the practice, at any rate in special cases, since he found a rhetorician to teach his son from the early age of eleven.

3

THE CHIEF purpose of the *de Oratore* was to shew that the instruction given in the schools of rhetoric at Rome was an insufficient preparation for real oratory. We may note in passing that the blame for this rested chiefly on the Romans themselves; the teachers were Greeks, who followed the technical methods of their own country, which, though excellent on the formal side, were far removed from Roman experience and to a great extent foreign to Roman ideas. As early as 92 B.C. steps had been taken officially to suppress the *Latini rhetores*, when the censors Cn. Domitius Ahenobarbus and L. Licinius Crassus published an edict against the Schools of Latin rhetoricians, on the ground that they were undesirable and contrary to ancestral tradition. Crassus, himself the chief speaker in the dialogue now in question, is made to defend his action on the ground that the Latin teachers were incompetent. Whatever the reason, the Latin teachers, though they cannot have been altogether suppressed, made little headway until the time of Vespasian, who endowed a chair of Latin rhetoric, of which Quintilian was the first holder.

"No one," says Cicero, "can hope to be an orator in the true sense of the word unless he has acquired knowledge of all the sciences and all the great problems of life." [9] Rhetoric is to be a part of the training, and a not unimportant one; Cicero himself studied it all through his life: but it is subordinate to the rest. The orator must have traversed the whole field of knowledge.[10] Theoretically, as he will be called upon to deal with all sorts of cases, he must have knowledge of a very great variety of subjects, which Cicero enumerates; but as universal knowledge is unattainable, he decides to deal with those subjects which are of so much practical importance as to be indispensable. The chief of these are history, jurisprudence, and philosophy; but it is taken for granted that the orator will have received the ordinary preliminary education, on a wide basis, already referred to; he will have studied the 'liberal arts' so far as they are taught at school.

The reference to history points to a noticeable gap in ordinary Roman education; this subject was certainly taught to some extent by the *grammaticus,* probably by means of lectures. Cato, we know, wrote a history-book for his own son, but there were no text-books in general use in the time of Cicero. The study of such poets as Ennius and Naevius might give the pupils a general idea of the sequence of events, but prose-writers were not studied in school, and even if they had been, Roman historians, as Cicero himself remarks, were sadly deficient in the qualities which he would like to find in history. "The first law of history," he says, "is not to dare to say anything that is false; the second, not to dare to suppress anything that is true." [11] It is strange that the Romans, who attached such importance to ancestral custom, paid comparatively little attention to the careful study of events on which their noble traditions were founded. Some knowledge of the subject was assumed in the rhetorical schools, though it was not taught there, for themes taken from Roman history were occasionally set for declamatory exercise; but such subjects seem to have been outnumbered by those taken from Greek history, mythology, and even romance.

The characters in Cicero's dialogue go on to debate the question whether the orator can be an expert in law, and Antonius declares against the possibility, but Cicero held that some study of it at least was necessary. The experience of several generations had proved that the best jurists were not the best pleaders, and the best orators were often almost ignorant of the subject. Finally, the true orator must have a philosophic outlook, for, like the preliminary studies, but in a higher sense, philosophy supplies material for oratory. To this end philosophy must be deeply and carefully studied, as Cicero himself had studied it. But a mere technical familiarity with philosophical dogmas is not enough; the best philosopher may not be a good speaker. The orator possesses the philosopher's knowledge and outlook, and the rhetorician's skill, but he is something higher than either. Cicero considers that he learned his oratory in the groves of Academus; but without his training in the rhetorical school of Molon he might have been inarticulate. His conclusions may be regarded as a liberal interpretation of Cato's views — the orator is *vir bonus dicendi peritus*, said Cato; by the 'good man' Cicero understood the 'philosopher.'

Cicero, both by precept and example, teaches us how much higher a thing is oratory than mere rhetoric; but he is the last of the true Roman orators.

B. QUINTILIAN [*ca.* 35–*ca.* 118 A.D.]

4

IN THE century which followed Cicero's death, several writers touched on the question of education, though they did not go deeply into the matter. Seneca the Elder was the champion of Ciceronianism at the time when the tide of popular opinion had turned against it; Vitruvius insisted on the necessity of a sound general education for an architect, and proposed a list of 'liberal arts' which he thought necessary as preliminary studies: "Neither talent without training nor training without talent can produce the perfect artist. A man who proposes to become an architect must be educated in literature, skilful with his pencil, expert in geometry; he must have made a general survey of history, and have carefully studied philosophy; he must know his music, have some knowledge of medicine, and be familiar with law, astronomy, and the principles which govern the heavens."[12] This is probably nothing more than traditional conservatism on the part of Vitruvius, whose views are sound though his justification of them is feeble. Under the early Empire liberty, both of speech and action, was restricted in many ways, but a high place was still assigned to oratory, and towards the end of the first century Quintilian, an authorized teacher of Latin rhetoric, propounded his views on *The Education of an Orator* (*Institutio Oratoria*).

Fortunately for us he held, in contrast to most writers on the subject, that the way in which the twig is bent will determine the growth of the tree; and where others had been used to take for granted the studies pursued in early stages before the pupil came under the tuition of the *rhetor,* he considers that nothing, however trivial, should be neglected. While setting before himself the Ciceronian ideal of the orator, he is not content to tell us merely what should be the course of higher studies leading to its attainment, but considers education as a whole from the very beginning.

Of the twelve books into which his treatise

is divided, the first is concerned with elementary education, starting from early childhood, the second with the proper content of education in a school of rhetoric. Books III to XI are mainly concerned with the *technique* of rhetoric, except for a famous digression on Latin Literature. The XIIth book contains a theoretical discussion of the higher studies which the orator should pursue after he has finished the rhetorical course. For our present purpose we shall find the first two books the most interesting. Other authors, both Greek and Roman, had written good handbooks of rhetoric; Quintilian was the first to tackle scientifically the wider problem of general education.

5

QUINTILIAN tells us in his admirable preface to Book I that his aim is the education of the perfect orator. The first essential is that he should be a good man, possessing exceptional powers of speech and every moral excellence. The ideal orator is a good citizen who can be relied on to manage any public or private business, to guide the State by his counsels, establish it by his legislation, and correct it by his judgements. The study of moral philosophy is therefore an inseparable accompaniment to the study of oratory.

The ideal orator must have a claim to the name of philosopher in the highest sense — for Quintilian notes in passing that the meaning of the word has been of late years degraded — and in addition to a blameless character, which is not in itself sufficient, he must be well versed in the theory and practice of speaking. Perfect eloquence is not beyond the reach of human intellect, and though few of us may attain it, those who aspire to the highest will climb further than those who halt at the foot of the ascent.

6

AFTER this statement of his aims, Quintilian attacks the problem of early education from the beginning.[13] All, or nearly all human beings have a natural proclivity to learning. Those who are incapable of profiting by education are abnormal, and as rare as monstrous births. Talent may vary in degree, but failure is more often due to lack of care than lack of ability. The father should entertain the highest hopes for his son from the moment of birth.

Parents should be as highly educated as possible, both fathers and mothers; and if they have not been fortunate in this matter they should do all the more to give their children what they themselves have missed. The first care is to see that the nurse chosen speaks correctly and is of good character; for childish impressions are retained throughout life, just as the scent of the roses will cling to the jar. Moreover, bad habits, so easily acquired, are more lasting than good. Next, the *paedagogus* should, if possible, be an educated man, or if not, he should realize his lack of education.

As opposed to those who think that children should not learn to read till they are seven years old, Quintilian would have them begin much earlier; but lessons in infancy should be more like play, lest the child should come to hate them. He must be encouraged by praise when he has done well, he must engage in competition with others, and must have prizes suitable to his age.[14]

The common practice of teaching the names and order of the letters of the alphabet sooner than their shape is condemned; children must learn the names and shapes of individual letters just as they do those of persons. The recent experiment of giving them ivory letters to play with is excellent because it amuses and teaches them at the same time. When the letters have been learned, writing may begin. To accustom the child to forming the letters properly, they may be at first deeply incised in a board, and the learner may then follow their shapes with a stilus before he attempts to reproduce them independently. The sounds of syllables (i.e., letters in combination) must next be learned by heart, and then we may proceed to reading, always remembering that undue haste defeats its own purpose, so reading must be slow and sure. 'Copies' to be written should not be meaningless collections of words, but should convey useful moral lessons. The sayings of famous men, and, above all, selections from poetry, may be committed to memory; for children love poetry, and at an early age memory is the only faculty which can be developed by teaching.[15]

It is remarkable that Quintilian is in favour of giving early instruction in Greek rather than in Latin; it must not, however, be continued long enough to spoil Latin pronunciation.[16]

We are next to face the question whether it is better for boys to be educated at school or at home. It is often urged that at school they are likely to be exposed to corrupting influences and learn bad habits; but Quintilian points out that bad habits are just as likely to be picked up at home; the examples of the elders are often bad, and children are constantly pampered and spoiled. Whereas some urge the great advantage to be obtained from having the sole attention of a well-qualified teacher, it is pointed out that the boy does not want individual attention all the time, and the boy brought up at home may become a shy recluse, whereas in a school he will from the first learn how to behave in a society — a lesson of the utmost importance for his later career. Further, boys learn from imitating each other, just as much as they learn from a master. School gives the greatest incentive to study, namely emulation. When Quintilian himself went to school the boys of each class were arranged in order, and the order changed every month; to be top of the form was a much coveted honour for which all competed seriously. A further point not to be neglected is that the child has the opportunity of forming friendships which may sometimes last throughout life. The decision then, is in favour of school education, but the school should be carefully chosen. The classes must not be too large, and the master must be capable of studying the character of each individual and adapting his lessons to the capacity of each. A narrow-necked vessel cannot be filled if you pour the liquid in too fast; you must pour slowly, or even instil learning drop by drop in some cases.[17]

The practice of flogging is condemned as brutalizing and ineffective.[18] Sufficient opportunity should be allowed for play; occasional holidays are desirable, for boys work better after a rest, but they must not be of so frequent occurrence as to make the boys think that work is only an interruption of play.[19]

Much of Quintilian's theory may seem commonplace to us, but nevertheless it is of permanent practical value. What makes the early part of his treatise attractive is the sound common sense which characterizes it, and the fact that he is superior to any of his predecessors in his understanding of the psychology of the child's mind. The remainder of the first book contains discussions on grammar, for which the writer was an enthusiast, on the correct use of words, orthography and pronunciation — all of them interesting to students of language. Composition and other studies necessary for rhetoric come in for due treatment. The second book deals chiefly with preliminary rhetorical studies and the distinction between rhetoric and oratory.

7

THE MORE thoroughly technical part of the work begins in Book III, with an apology for the dryness of the subject. With the technical details of the science to which he devotes so much space we are not here concerned, but we may conclude by emphasizing his defence of Ciceronian principles, both as to the definition of the orator and the nature of the subjects which he must study. We may note finally that Quintilian was not merely an academic teacher of technique, but a practical man also, who had, as he himself tells us, had experience as a successful pleader in the law-courts.

Quintilian, like many other distinguished literary men of the early Empire, was a native of Spain. Born at Calagurris (Callahorra) in 35 A.D., the son of a rhetorician who had practised in Rome, he was sent to Rome to be educated, and subsequently returned to teach rhetoric in his native land. In 68 A.D. he was brought back to Rome by Galba, and established a school in which he taught for twenty years. He was the first Latin rhetorician to receive official recognition and a state-salary, being appointed to a 'chair' founded by Vespasian. The *Institutio Oratoria* was written by him fairly late in life, when at last, as he says, after twenty years spent in the training of the young, he obtained leisure for study.[20] He died not much later than 100 A.D. and with his death an important period of Roman Education may be said to close.

VI. THE EMPIRE

I

AT THE close of the Republican era practically the whole of Italy was Romanized — to the extent, at least, that the civilization and education throughout the peninsula were uniform. There was now no distinction in political status between the various cities which in earlier times had been divided into several classes according to their degrees of privilege.

The conquests of Julius Caesar had firmly established Roman civilization in vast districts beyond the Alps, and the policy instituted by him of extending the Roman citizenship to peoples beyond the limits of Italy commended itself to successive Emperors. Roman ideas and Roman culture spread so rapidly that before the close of the first century we find Martial recording a long list of names of men distinguished in literature who were not Roman born, and a Gallic poet of the fifth century can regard the whole civilized world as part of Rome.[1]

As Rome herself spread over countries which had in earlier days been regarded as barbarous, so the barbarians of all kinds began steadily to flow into Italy and Rome; the extent of civilization increased, and Rome was no longer the only centre. It had been said in jest of Caesar that he made senators of men who could not speak Latin, but the jest very soon lost its point, if it ever had one, for Roman education was the first instrument of civilization. The education which spread over the West, as it had already dominated the East independently of Roman influence, was of the rhetorical type described by Quintilian and developed under the influence of debased Greek practice. As in the Scipionic age, Greece had once more taken the conqueror captive.

To Cicero, oratory was the highest education, and other studies were valuable in so far as they contributed to the equipment of the perfect orator. As far as words go, the ideals of Quintilian were very similar; but we must take into account the different circumstances under which these two great teachers lived.

Living in the last days of the Republic, with

the great republican traditions behind him, Cicero conceived of the orator as a man of practical wisdom and trained intellect, capable not only of giving sound advice on matters of public interest, but also of impressing his opinions on the people, as Cicero was himself.

2

WITH the passing of Republican institutions the opportunity for exercising the highest gifts of the orator in the noblest way was gone. The rule of the Princeps gave no scope for the highest flights of deliberative oratory in the Senate-house or the forum, and the opportunities for its use even in the law-courts were much restricted. But the Roman character was essentially conservative, and still clung to the old forms when the old spirit was dead. The Roman gentleman must still aim at becoming a potential orator, though he might never practise his art in public. Thus the curriculum of grammar and rhetoric was retained, and the technicalities of rhetoric came to be the only end of education. Other subjects were studied only as subsidiary to rhetoric, and they inevitably suffered. The value of history, science, mathematics, and other branches of learning was that they could provide 'common-places' for the use of the rhetorician. We find, under the early Empire, that compendiums of historical incidents were compiled to provide the student with illustrations and topics; the known, or supposed, facts of science were accepted without question by succeeding generations, and little advance was made in general knowledge. The strength of tradition precluded enquiry or innovation, and authority was as strong as it was later, in the days of Scholasticism. Rhetoric dominated not only the literature but even the life of the Roman world.

With the growth of the Empire these rhetorical ideals of education spread over the world. The West was from the outset particularly eager to acquire Roman culture. Not many years after the conquests of Julius Caesar an important rhetorical school had come into existence at Autun; under Tiberius, the sons of the Gallic nobility flocked to its class-rooms.[2] After his successful campaigns in Britain the first care of Agricola was to induce the natives to study the liberal arts; he played on their vanity, says Tacitus, by telling them that they were more apt at learning than their kinsmen the Gauls, and the result was that this nation, which had hitherto despised and avoided the Latin language, soon produced enthusiastic students of rhetoric. The conquest begun by the sword was completed by the tongue.[3]

Juvenal foreshadows the Romanization of the world by exclaiming that Thule is proposing to find a salary for a *rhetor*,[4] and the Gaul Rutilius is thinking partly of the conquest by culture when he says: *Urbem fecisti quod prius orbis erat.* Among the professors of Bordeaux recorded by Ausonius (310–*ca.*395 A.D.) we find, side by side with Romans, the son of a Druid and a priest of the Gallic deity Belenus.[5] Throughout the provinces, Spain, Africa, even in such semi-civilized districts as Dacia, the same influence was at work. Roman education followed close behind the flight of the Roman eagles, just as Hellenism trod on the heels of Alexander in his victorious progress.

3

THE CHIEF centre of culture in Gaul during Republican times was the Greek town of Massilia, the ally of Rome in the second Punic War, which long maintained the traditional friendship. Here Greek influence remained predominant, and Strabo gives a striking account of its influence: "All people of culture there," he writes, "turn to oratory and philosophy. A short while ago this city was left as a school for barbarians, and produced such a love of Greek among the Gauls that they even wrote their contracts in Greek. Now, however, it has tempted even the most distinguished Romans, who wish to study, to go there instead of to Athens to attend courses."[6] By using the phrase παιδευτήριον 'the school of Gaul,' Strabo at least implies that the Greek influence of Marseilles was widespread. But Suetonius (born *ca.*75 A.D.) speaks of Roman rhetors also penetrating into the provinces, particularly into Gallia Togata, and mentions several names of rhetors, the earliest being Cato Grammaticus, who were of Gallic origin.[7] It is significant that in Tacitus' *Dialogus* all the speakers, with one exception, are Gauls. Through the second and third centuries education in Gaul continued to flourish, almost every important town having a school of rhetoric and producing teachers of its own.

Civil disorder, barbarian inroads, and the repressive measures of such enemies of learning as Caracalla, disorganized the system, but fresh stimulus was provided by the able and enlightened Constantius Chlorus, father of Constantine the Great, who, becoming governor of Gaul in 292 A.D., gave active encouragement to education. Massilia, however, the centre of Greek influence in the South, was now on the decline; Autun, the great Latin University of the North, had recently been sacked by barbarians; and the outlook for education was unpromising.

The fourth century was a period of peace for Gaul which contributed to the revival of literary studies. It was now that Bordeaux, the home of Ausonius, rose to prominence and eclipsed the earlier fame of Autun. During this and the following century we have ample evidence that the Gauls, at any rate those of the upper classes, continued to take an interest in education which their gradual conversion to Christianity did not diminish. A large number of men who were prominent as leaders of Christian thought owed much of their authority to their pagan education.[8]

The Frankish invasion practically ended the tradition of the Roman schools in Gaul. They were succeeded in the fifth century by the monastic schools, which aimed at a religious education and were on the whole hostile to pagan learning. The cathedral-schools which followed them were equally unsatisfactory, and when Charlemagne wanted a head for his school of liberal arts he had to go to England, where the old ideals had persisted, and invite Alcuin of York to take charge of the education of the sons of his nobility.

4

WE MUST now turn back once more to the Greek-speaking world.

In the latter part of the first century A.D. oratory, which, during the Macedonian period, had been mainly devoted to display, showed a tendency to come once more into close relation with public life. Many Greek-speaking communities, in Asia Minor and elsewhere, retained, under Roman rule, some sort of independence, and kept their own local government under traditional forms. Instruction in oratory was the province of the Sophists, who unlike the Greek Sophists of the fifth century B.C. made no pretence at imparting a general culture, but resembled more the baser sort described by Isocrates, and aimed chiefly at a systematic teaching of rhetoric in relation to public life. A general interest in Greek studies had been fostered by the Emperors Claudius and Nero; [9] Vespasian went further, and endowed chairs of Greek and Latin rhetoric at Rome; [10] Nerva and Trajan are mentioned as having had personal friendship with famous Greek Sophists; [11] and Hadrian was so enthusiastic for Greek culture that he instituted a national assembly of Greek cities, to meet at Athens under the title of *Panhellenia*.[12] He gave certain immunities from taxation to philosophers, rhetors, physicians, and grammarians. In this practice he was followed by Antoninus Pius, who made elaborate regulations as to the number of Sophists, grammarians, and physicians who might thus be honoured in cities of various classes throughout the Empire.[13]

From the time of Vespasian onwards we have records of edicts by various emperors on the subject of professional salaries. It seems probable that the emperors as a rule did not spend their own money in this direction. Higher education was not a branch of the Imperial Civil Service; the salaries had to be found by the municipal authorities in each case, and the successive enactments imply that the townships were inclined to shirk their responsibilities.[14]

However Marcus Aurelius seems to have endowed out of the *fiscus* a second chair of rhetoric at Athens, where one already existed. Further, he made provision there for the appointment of salaried teachers in every branch of literary study.[15] University education was thus definitely established at Athens by the end of the second century A.D., and other institutions of learning flourished in many Greek towns of Asia, such as Smyrna, Ephesus, Tarsus, and Antioch. In all of these sophistry held the first place, and the interest in the rhetorical education given by the Sophists was almost world-wide.

Later emperors in some cases exercised direct control over education. Constantius Chlorus in the late third century fixed the salary to be paid to Eumenius, head of the school of Autun.[16] Constantine issued three edicts continuing the policy of his predecessors in conferring privileges on teachers of liberal arts.[17] Julian in 362 A.D. claimed the right to revise the appointments to professorships, in which hitherto the Emperor had rarely interfered, the matter being in the hands of the *curia* of each University.[18]

In this reign we find the question of religious disabilities first raised, by Julian's edict that no Christian should teach Greek.[19] This had no permanent result. The edict of Gratian in 376 A.D. left the towns free to appoint their own teachers, but fixed the salaries.[20] The importance still attached to rhetoric is shewn by the fact that the rhetorician's salary was twice as great as that of the teachers of 'grammar,' whether Latin or Greek. Finally an edict of Theodosius and Valentinian in 425 A.D. forbade the opening of schools by persons unauthorized by the government.[21]

In imperial times there was no system of general public education, but some emperors interested themselves in the requirements of the poorer classes. Thus Trajan undertook to provide education for five thousand orphans and children of needy citizens; Hadrian and the Antonines carried the same institution into the provinces, and Alexander Severus provided bursaries for poor scholars in some rhetorical schools.[22]

5

THE TEACHING was two-sided. On the one hand the Sophist took his pupils in the classroom, instructed them in the principles of rhetoric, set them exercises to write on definite themes, and afterwards corrected and improved their essays. On the other hand, the teacher would, at certain intervals, himself give public or semi-public displays, delivering an oration which might be deliberative or judicial or merely an encomium. These exhibitions were sometimes given at the request of a magistrate or other dignitary; sometimes even by royal command, as when the Emperor Marcus Aurelius, on visiting Smyrna, invited the rhetor Aristides to speak before him.[23] Aristides refused to do so without due notice. "It is not my way," he said, "to vomit my speeches; I need time to perfect them. Propose a theme today, and come to hear me tomorrow; and please allow my students to be in the audience." "Certainly," said Marcus, "for that is democratic." When the Sophist continued, "Give them leave, my lord, to shout and applaud as loudly as they can," the Emperor smiled, and replied, "That depends on you."

It was this Aristides whose eloquence induced Marcus to rebuild Smyrna, when the city had been destroyed by an earthquake.[24] Other sophists, however, were always ready to speak *extempore*. Hippodromus of Thessaly was specially noted for his smooth and fluent style in impromptu speaking. The subject was in some cases chosen by the audience, so that the sophist had to extemporize; but the experienced speaker, with the technicalities of his art at his finger-tips, his head stored with commonplaces and historical and mythological illustrations, would seldom be at a loss for words.[25]

From the writings of Libanius (314–393 A.D.) and Gregory Nazianzen (329–390 A.D.) we may form some picture of University life in the fourth century.

Libanius of Antioch was twenty-two years old when he went to Athens. This was somewhat above the usual age, but he had already begun his studies in his native city. At this time considerable rivalry existed among different sophists, each of whom had a body of students attached to him. These student-corps were organized under leaders, and co-operated to promote their masters' and their own interests. To some extent they were national, like the 'nations' of the mediaeval universities, for a stranger coming to Athens would tend to join the classes of a teacher of his own nationality, if such were to be found.[26]

The students sometimes paraded the streets to obtain recruits for their own bodies. A new-comer might be taken prisoner, and subjected to a considerable amount of banter and some mild ragging, which was alarming at first sight but was really good-humoured. Finally the neophyte was led in procession through the market-place and conducted to the bath, with which the initiation ceremony concluded. It was sometimes followed by a feast.[27]

A less pleasant feature was the rioting which occurred from time to time between rival bodies of students; free fights with clubs and stones took place in the streets; the populace took sides, and it was unsafe for any decent citizen to walk out of doors.[28] The sophists themselves might be drawn into the trouble, for if they appeared in public on these occasions they were liable to be mobbed and insulted.[29] It was often necessary for the civil authorities to interfere to check the disorder, fines and imprisonment being the punishment for the rioters.[30]

VII. THE MIDDLE AGES AND AFTER

I

THE SPREAD of Christianity had to some extent modified the course of education, for the Church on the whole was antagonistic to the dissemination of pagan learning. This is intelligible if we realize the conservatism of superstition and the conditions under which thousands of converts were enrolled under the new faith. In a later age Clovis, who consented to be baptized in gratitude for a victory, cannot have shaken himself entirely free from the old beliefs; his soldiers, who merely followed their leader's example, acted under compulsion rather than from conviction. When Constantine made Christianity the official religion, the great mass of the people in the Roman Empire must have turned from one worship to another as lightly as mercenaries transferring their allegiance, after a battle, to the winning side.

But polytheism died hard; to the minds of

the common people the ancient gods had been merely driven into exile by a superior power, and throughout the middle ages we find legends of the pagan deities appearing in some disguise or other; and, in fact, to popular orthodoxy, Pan, Bacchus, and other such divinities continued for centuries to exist, not as mythological abstractions, but as malignant spirits or demons. A creed which ascribed a personal existence to Satan was quite consistent in admitting the survival of the 'gods in exile.'

Thus, as a general rule, the Church was inclined to ban the study of any literature in which the pagan gods and religion were honoured. The opposition did not die out with the decay of mediaevalism: the later Church, down perhaps to the seventeenth century, objected to the moral tone of classical writers. But on the other hand many of the prominent figures in the early Church had, before their conversion, won distinction as professors of pagan learning, particularly in the schools of rhetoric, and could not shake off the influence of the studies which had provided their chief mental food up to or beyond middle age.[1] Further, the chief object of the Church was the study and interpretation of the Bible, which was not generally accessible in any of the vulgar tongues; so that it was necessary from the first for the Christian apologists to be well versed in the study of Latin, in order to understand the Vulgate; while those who had some knowledge of Greek were at a still greater advantage for the exposition of doctrine. Knowledge of the classical languages could hardly be separated from some knowledge of classical literature. Thus mediaeval education was of twofold origin; as we have indicated, the machinery of education was organized and controlled by the Church by means of cathedral-schools, monastic institutions, and, later, to a great extent by Universities; but pagan traditions determined the greater part of the curriculum for many centuries, and still continue to influence it.

From the earliest times the Church was not unanimous; St. Jerome (340–420 A.D.), himself a pupil of Aelius Donatus, author of a Latin primer (the 'Donat') which, with all its incredible faults of arrangement and contents, remained in use as a school book for some ten centuries or more, persisted in the study of Latin, perhaps with some misgivings, on account of its great utility. Augustine, Bishop of Hippo (354–430 A.D.), was a professor of rhetoric at Milan before his conversion, and did not forget or repudiate his early studies; and though we find Pope Gregory (590–604 A.D.) reprimanding a bishop of Vienne for encouraging the teaching of 'grammar,' and thus countenancing the 'vanities of secular learning,'[2] a century later even the study of Greek was encouraged by Theodore of Tarsus, Archbishop of Canterbury from 668 to 690, and by the Abbot Hadrian.[3] Later still, under the care of Alcuin, the library of the Cathedral school at York contained a fine collection of standard Latin authors, including Virgil, Lucan, Pliny, and Statius, in addition to several of the Latin Fathers. Secular influence was also exerted from time to time. In England, great importance must be attached to the example and precept of the scholar-king Alfred; on the continent we find Charlemagne urging monks and priests to improve their Latin for the better understanding of the Scriptures.[4] In 782 Alcuin left York upon Charlemagne's invitation to organize education at the Frankish court.

2

THE CONTENT of education was the 'Seven Liberal Arts' which are first mentioned as such under this title by Martianus Capella, a pagan rhetorician of Carthage, in the early part of the fifth century. They were divided into the *Trivium* and the *Quadrivium*. The Trivium consisted of grammar, dialectic, and rhetoric, grammar being widely interpreted as the study of language and literature. The Quadrivium, first mentioned under that name by Boethius (480–524) comprised music, arithmetic, geometry, and astronomy.

The rhetorical schools of the Roman Empire left a deep impression on the educational systems of the Middle Ages, although the foundation and organization of schools and Universities in Europe was due to the Christian Church. However much the Church distrusted pagan education, a knowledge of Latin was essential to all who could study the origins and history of the Faith, and the Latin writers were even more important for students of secular subjects, since they were the repositories of law, history, mathematics, science, in fact of all practical knowledge. The best approach to these storehouses of information was by the traditional path of the grammatical and rhetorical school, based on the linguistic study of the Classics; so that pagan, as well as Christian, writers of Latin works, were inevitably retained as textbooks.

3

THE HOSTILITY between pagan education and Christianity was not acute at first, when the adherents of the new faith were mostly of humble origin; it only assumed serious proportions when men of high position and culture were drawn into the Church. Some of the early Fathers, as we have seen, took a liberal view, that Christian theology was the culmination of philosophy; others, while bitterly opposed to the pagan education because it was so closely incorporated with pagan traditions and practices, recognized the necessity of learning from the enemy in order that they might meet him with his own weapons. St. Augustine and St. Jerome took the reasonable view that literary culture was a good thing so long as it could be subordinated to Christian principles.

One reason for the survival of rhetoric was, perhaps, that it was entirely intellectual, and involved no moral teaching which might have come into conflict with Christian ethics; but even so, the pagan ideals of individualism and self-reliance were definitely opposed to the

Christian principles of humility and self-negation which found their consummation in monasticism.

From the fifth to the ninth centuries the gradual encroachments of the barbarians, who, though they admired the culture of the Empire, were hardly capable of assimilating it, and did little to preserve it, caused a temporary eclipse of Classical learning, which was, however, kept alive in a few isolated monasteries, particularly in Britain and Ireland. The enthusiasm of Charlemagne, and the loyal energy of his adviser Alcuin, brought about a revival of letters which partially, at any rate, survived the difficult times ensuing on the death of the Frankish king. The monastic schools which were established throughout the Empire were of supreme importance, since every monastery, in addition to teaching ecclesiastics, had provision for the education of external students who had no intention of taking orders or vows. The basis of education was still the Seven liberal arts.

4

THE ELEVENTH century is marked by the beginning of a new movement, Scholasticism, based on the re-discovery of the works of Aristotle, which became known first through translations into Latin of Arabic versions obtained from the East or from Moorish Spain, and later by direct translations from the Greek original. Dialectic was a powerful instrument in the hands of men like Abélard (1079–1142) who devoted themselves to logical investigation of the fundamental doctrines of the Church. The weakness of Scholastic education was a tendency to hurry over the early cultural elements in order to approach metaphysical problems without delay, and further, to regard the ancients as the ultimate authority on natural phenomena — a fault which was repeated by the scholars of the Renaissance. Nevertheless, modern Science may be said to have begun during this period, with the researches of Roger Bacon (1214–1294). The most signal service done to the world by Scholasticism was the institution of Universities, which came into being spontaneously in Italy, France, and England, through the congregation of students who flocked to the towns to attach themselves to some learned teacher. At a later time royal or ecclesiastical charters were granted to such bodies of students and teachers, confirming the rights of self-organization which they had already assumed; and still later, Universities began to be founded either by civic or other higher authority.

Many analogies may be found between the mediaeval universities and those of the ancient world. Students were attracted from all parts of Europe to Paris or Bologna by the fame of some particular teacher, just as in earlier days they had flocked to Athens or Antioch to enrol themselves under some famous philosopher or sophist; but this only amounts to saying that similar results, in different ages, will follow similar causes. The University of the Middle Ages can trace no direct descent from the philosophical or sophistical schools; its only inheritance was the dry bones of an old-fashioned curriculum — the 'liberal arts' — which required the inspiration of Humanism to rehabilitate them in a living form.

5

THE DECLINE of Scholasticism, with its arid metaphysical speculations, gave an opportunity for renewed interest in Latin and Greek studies. It is arbitrary to fix any date for the beginning of the new movement. Dante (1265–1321) was a devoted student of Virgil, but we are not to believe that he re-discovered the works of the great Mantuan. Petrarch (1304–1374) has a considerable claim to be regarded as the greatest of the early champions of the revival of Greek studies. The patronage of the Medici at Florence in the early fifteenth century gave a great stimulus to all branches of culture, and especially to the revival of Greek learning which, flourishing first in Italy, spread rapidly through Europe till it produced a definite change in the type of international culture. The Renaissance was many-sided, and education was only one of the ways in which the new spirit manifested itself, but it is the only one with which we are directly concerned, and it is interesting to see how far classical traditions predominated.

Theorists of this period were greatly influenced by Quintilian's *Institutio Oratoria* and by a treatise *On the education of children* (πρεὶ παίδων ἀγωγῆς), falsely ascribed to Plutarch (*ca.* 100 A.D.). The former of these works has been dealt with in an earlier chapter; the latter is chiefly concerned with the moral aspect of education. Virtue is regarded as the best of possessions, and education the best means of attaining it; morals and manners are of supreme importance; physical exercises, especially those connected with military training, are to be encouraged, and a general education on the traditional classical lines is recommended. The highest of intellectual studies is philosophy, and the happiest man is he who can combine this study with service to the State. Little is said about details of educational method, but like Quintilian, the author of this treatise regards education chiefly as having a practical end, and any system based on such foundations must from the first be at variance with the theological ideals of the middle ages.

6

THE HUMANISTIC educators of the fifteenth century emphasized the importance of the practical side of education. The aim of Vittorino da Feltre was to develop the complete citizen, and in this he is in accord with other writers from the outset of the humanistic period.[5] There is a marked tendency, on the one hand, to individualism, but the learned individual must not retire to a cloister; he should frequent the city and shun solitude, thinking of the good of the community no less than of his own personal distinction.

A liberal education is, according to Vergerius, one which develops the highest gifts of body and mind. Moral worth and reputation, rather than gain or pleasure, should be the aim of a lofty nature.[6] Aeneas Silvius Piccolomini (afterwards Pope Pius II) was a man of action, concerned more with life than with study. He regarded geometry as a better training than dialectic, and quoted with approval the case of Archimedes: but Humanism's claim was so strong that in writing the treatise *De liberorum educatione* (A.D. 1450) to Ladislas, the boy-king of Bohemia, he insisted on the educational value of Letters, without which philosophy, so necessary to a prince, is hardly intelligible: "Literature is our guide to the true meaning of the past, to a proper estimate of the present, to a sound forecast of the future." Thus, not only for the statesman, but for members of the learned professions, and even for merchants of the higher class, literary education was regarded, during the fifteenth century, as the best passport to success. This respect for antiquity was in some cases carried to absurd lengths: it was not merely that the study of ancient literature provided a good mental and moral training, but that the works of the ancients must be considered as authoritative on practical detail. Aristotle's *Politics* was the best handbook of statecraft, Caesar's *Commentaries* were the basis of military science, and Virgil's *Georgics,* of agriculture.[7]

To train the good citizen was, as we have seen, the ideal of the fifteenth century thinkers, and thus it would be to some extent the duty of the State to interest itself in the training of the younger generation. Control should be exercized chiefly on the moral side; but in order to serve the community best, the individual must be developed as far as his nature will allow. The earlier humanists, such as da Feltre, probably did not realize the possibility of any conflict between the humanistic and the Christian life; Vittorino himself never departed in the slightest degree from his duty as a Christian; but the emphasis laid on the importance of the individual in relation to the State rather than to the Church was bound in the end to lead to an antagonism.

7

THE CHIEF educational leaders of the early period were men who had been brought up under the shadow of Scholasticism, but had broken away from it. Vittorino da Feltre entered the University of Padua at the age of eighteen, in the year 1396 A.D., the very year in which Manuel Chrysoloras of Constantinople was invited by the 'Studium' of Florence to become the first professor of Greek in the West. Padua, where the memory of Petrarch was still a living force, already shewed signs of breaking with scholastic tradition, even in such subjects as dialectic and theology, and the ground for Humanism was well prepared.

Vittorino remained at Padua, as student and teacher, for twenty years; his main interest was the Arts course, comprising Latin Grammar and Literature, Rhetoric, Dialectic, and Moral Philosophy; but he also, after graduating, took courses in Mathematics and in Canon Law. He maintained himself by working as a Grammar-master and giving private lessons in Mathematics. For the last eight years of his residence he was in close touch with Barzizza, the greatest Latin scholar of the time, who came to Padua as professor of Rhetoric in 1407. Up to 1415 Vittorino had no opportunity of learning Greek, but in that year he migrated to Venice, to join Guarino, who had recently opened a School there. This man, who had lived some years in the household of Chrysoloras, could write and speak Greek, an accomplishment shared at most by two or three Italian scholars of the time. Under his guidance Vittorino worked with unremitting zeal for eighteen months and acquired a knowledge of Greek which greatly enhanced his already considerable reputation for scholarship.[8]

In 1422 he consented, with some reluctance, to accept the offer of the Chair of Rhetoric at Padua. This he resigned a year or two later owing to the disorderly state of the University, and returned to Venice, where he opened a school, chiefly for the sons of Venetian nobles. In 1423 he was invited by Gonzaga, who wanted a humanist of distinction to educate his children, to migrate to Mantua. This offer he accepted, and remained at Mantua till his death in 1426.

His first care was the instruction of the Gonzaga children, but from the beginning a few children of the Mantuan nobility were added to the school; later on, Vittorino accepted others who were specially recommended to him, ranging from sons of princes to boys so poor that the Master received and entertained them entirely free of charge.

The Lord of Mantua set apart a beautiful house surrounded with gardens, near his own place, for the use of the School. Games and other healthy amusements were encouraged as relaxation between lessons; corporal punishment was very rare, and the master took the deepest personal interest in every one of his pupils.

The subject matter of education was mainly Greek and Latin Literature. The education of the time found no place for the study of Italian, which was regarded rather as a group of dialects than a language, convenient for the intercourse of daily life but of no value as a literary medium. Some of Dante's contemporaries regretted that he had chosen the vulgar tongue for his *Divina Commedia,*[9] and even insinuated that he did so on account of his ignorance of Latin. It was felt at that time that Latin must become the common language of the educated world; it was natural, then, for Vittorino to regard Latin as the proper medium of instruction.

The method of study was based upon the mediaeval Trivium and Quadrivium; but the difference in the relative importance now attached to the 'Seven liberal arts,' and the new angle from which the arts themselves were approached, constituted in fact a revolution. Such terms as Grammar, Rhetoric, Dialectic, and the rest were retained; but Grammar and Rhetoric taken together comprised not only linguistic study and composition in Greek and Latin, but an attempt to enter into the spirit and comprehend the thought of the ancient world by an absorption in its literature and history. Dialectic, which to the mediaeval mind was an end in itself, sank to a subordinate position. The proper subject of education was Letters, and all other subjects were subsidiary. Reading aloud was practised every day by the younger pupils, the master insisting on correctness, on proper emphasis, and on clear enunciation. Declamation of passages learnt by heart followed — first, short passages of Ovid and Horace, and, later, of the pupil's own compositions. Memory was constantly strengthened in this way. Eventually some boys and girls of fourteen could recite whole speeches of Cicero or Demosthenes and long passages of Homer and Virgil.[10] The school-hours, about seven a day, were divided among a considerable number of subjects, taught by a variety of masters who were selected for their special knowledge, so that the pupils should have the best of everything. Arithmetic was valued as a training in accuracy; geometry and algebra were taught in connection with drawing and surveying; natural philosophy and natural history found a place, and elementary astronomy was substituted for astrology, which at the time was still popular in some Universities. Vocal and instrumental music, and dancing, were admitted under careful restrictions.

In reading a passage from an author, Vittorino first explained the exact meaning of each word and its construction in the sentence; he then commented on the style of the writer as exemplified in the passage; lastly the allusions were explained. At each stage illustrations were given from parallel passages of the same author and others. Each pupil took notes which enabled him to compile his own vocabulary. Virgil held the first place among Latin authors; Ovid, Lucan, and Horace, together with Livy — the object of particular attention — Cicero, and Sallust were also frequently read.

In Greek the same methods were followed; Homer, Demosthenes, Xenophon, Arrian, and Herodotus were among the favourite authors;

Plato was read with the highest class. The parallel teaching of Latin and Greek was considered important, and the latter was begun, at any rate by promising pupils, at a much earlier age than is customary in modern times. Prose-composition in Greek and Latin was regularly practised, so that the pupils soon became proficient; they also learned to write Latin verse, particularly Virgilian hexameters.[11] The exercises were carefully corrected by Vittorino himself, who in Latin-composition insisted on adherence to Ciceronian standards.

Ancient history was studied chiefly from the ethical and practical standpoint, and thus Plutarch, whose *Lives* had a great influence on the thought of the period, was the favourite Greek author; of the Romans, Livy, Sallust, Q. Curtius, and Valerius Maximus were chiefly read.

Philosophy also was treated as a guide to practical life, and thus stress was laid on Ethics rather than Metaphysics. This was the highest course in the School, and Vittorino considered that those pupils who had passed through it would find themselves thoroughly well equipped for any public or professional career which they might subsequently choose to follow.

Such a conception of the value of a humanistic education has found echoes even amid the stress of modern times.[12]

Dialectic (or Logic), which was one of the four constituents of the Arts course of the Universities at this time, was never so popular in Italy as in other countries of Europe. The Italian mind revolted against the subtleties of sophistical disputation which characterized Oxford and Paris. Vittorino valued Logic merely as an aid to correct thought and exposition, and in this he was in accord with another great humanist, Vergerius, who, though himself a professor of Logic at Padua, maintained that he differed from other logicians in teaching the subject only as a guide to the study of other sciences.

8

WE HAVE TAKEN Vittorino as a typical educator of his time, with a view to shewing what humanistic education could do under favourable circumstances. He is typical of the spirit of his age in Italy, and this spirit is expressed in the writings of numerous theorists of the same epoch. Vergerius (1370–1444), already referred to as having broken away from scholastic methods in his teaching of Dialectic, composed a treatise *De ingenuis moribus* in which he laid down the principles on which humanistic education was to be established. Bruni d'Arezzo (1369–1444) addressed to the illustrious lady, Baptista Malatesta, a letter in which he expounded a system of study suitable for women. Aeneas Silvius (1405–1464) shews in his *De liberorum educatione* that, though more interested in practical affairs than in literature, he regarded a literary education on the lines of the new Learning as indispensable to a gentleman. Battista Guarino (son of the Guarino mentioned above—p. 170), in his treatise on the study of the Classical authors (1459), maintains the necessity of studying the literatures both of Greece and Rome; other subjects are of little importance to him.

These early humanists for the most part shew, both by precept and practice, that there is nothing inconsistent between pagan learning and Christian life; Vittorino was a deeply religious man; Bruni particularly recommends, among other subjects of study, the works of Christian writers. There are other points in which there is a general agreement. The schoolmaster, says Guarino, should be in the position of a father to his pupils — as, in fact, Vittorino was. He should be a man whom they can respect and love; who will guide them, without resorting to harsh and unreasonable punishments, and can study and know their characters individually. This is a noticeable contrast to the schoolmasters of Petrarch's day, who, we may believe, were common in most European countries — "men who are not happy unless they can terrify, flog and torture; cold blooded creatures of limited intelligence, who take up the profession from mercenary motives and because they are not capable of doing anything better." [13]

9

In Italy, education was fostered by the heads of reigning houses, who encouraged distinguished scholars to frequent their courts. Vittorino was better paid, and had more liberty of action, as a Court schoolmaster than as a University professor. Chiefly owing to the prevalence of such patronage it was thought more important to be the pupil of a famous humanist than to have a distinguished University record. Thus the new movement was able to spread quite independently of any action on the part of the Universities. In other countries the growth of the new Learning was slower, and in some cases the opposition to it was violent. Thus, at a time considerably later than that with which we have been dealing, when certain persons attempted to introduce the study of Greek at Oxford, a society called 'the Trojans' was formed for the express purpose of denouncing, vilifying, and in every way hindering the progress of such 'heresy.' Thomas More in 1518 wrote a letter of protest to the University authorities; Erasmus, writing a year later, records that the study of Greek at Cambridge proceeds without hindrance; but at Oxford the disturbance was so great that the King (Henry VIII), hearing of it from More, thought it desirable to intimate officially that those who wished to study Greek should be allowed to do so.[14] At Paris in 1517 a correspondent of Erasmus complains that he is bitterly disappointed at finding no opportunity for the study of Greek, whereas crowds of students attend the disputations of theological sophists.[15]

The opposition to the new movement was probably twofold; partly, the Universities resented any departure from their established curriculum, and, partly, theologians looked with suspicion on the supposed anti-Christian tendencies of Humanism. It was this more serious opposition that education had to face in Italy in the sixteenth century, but it existed to some extent in England. However, Colet, who mentions it in his letters,[16] established Greek as a subject to be taught in St. Paul's School, which he founded in 1509, though he was careful to shew by his statutes that the moral and Christian side of education was as important as the intellectual.[17]

VIII. CONCLUSION

I

MODERN education is so varied, and the sources from which its systems are derived are so numerous, that it is difficult to say exactly how much we owe, whether directly or indirectly, to the ancient world. Minor analogies may often be traced, but they are, as often as not, accidental; the differences are more strongly marked than the resemblances.

The debt of modern literature to the Classics is incalculable, chiefly owing to the fact that, since the Renaissance, there has been an unbroken tradition of Classical teaching in public schools for more than four hundred years. In addition to this, the value of the discipline involved in a strict training in Greek and Latin, and of the careful and orderly habits in writing and thought which this training produces, are of no slight importance. In modern times the most remarkable tribute to the importance of the Classics in education was paid by the speakers at the Conference on Classical Studies organized at Princeton by Dean A. F. West in 1917, and recorded by him in *The Value of the Classics.* Nearly three hundred prominent men, including statesmen, judges, lawyers, railroad presidents, professors of various sciences, schoolmasters and journalists, all testified to the importance of a classical training. Their judgement is borne out by tables of statistics shewing the superiority in various branches of study attained by classical over non-classical students.[1]

Though Greek has been, and continues to be, of the highest importance as an influence on the thought of the ages, Latin has played a greater part than Greek in the history of our education, chiefly from the fact that it persisted so long as a spoken language. For many centuries Latin was inevitably studied by the learned classes, whether priests or laymen. Long after it had ceased to be the language of Italy, it was still cultivated in some form as a living language. Montaigne, the famous author of the *Essays,* remarks that up to the age of seven he himself spoke only Latin, knowing no more of French or Perigordin than he did of Arabic.[2] Queen Elizabeth could make a fluent speech in Latin; Roger Ascham in the same age regrets the tendency of the times to begin the study of Latin too early, " for children by starting too soon only learn to speak it badly." [3]

The vitality of Latin is shewn by the fact that, till the beginning of the nineteenth century, it survived as a spoken language, at any rate in some English public schools,[4] and that down to a still later time editions of classical authors intended for the use of schoolboys were commonly provided with explanatory notes in Latin, and sometimes, if the author were a verse-writer, with a paraphrase in Latin prose.[5] As an international means of the communication of ideas Latin has never been superseded; it is the common medium of address employed by Universities and learned Societies of different nationalities in writing to each other, and is still the international language of certain learned publications, in the same way as it was in the days of Copernicus or Newton, who wrote in Latin, rather than in German or English, in order that their works might appeal to a wider public. The study of the language, thus persisting through the ages, necessarily involved some study of the institutions and traditions of the ancients, or, at least, put such study within the general reach.

2

If we look back on conditions of life in Ancient Greece and Rome we see at once that comparison with the present age is made difficult by the existence, in both ancient cases, of the institution of slavery. In Greek states a great proportion of labour, both unskilled and technical, was performed by slaves. Still more remarkable was the case of Rome, where not only manual labour but a considerable amount of highly skilled work, for instance in the secretarial branch, was entrusted to men of the slave-class, often well-born and educated Greeks or Asiatics, whom the fortune of war had placed at the disposal of their conquerors. Such men occasionally attained their freedom, and under the Empire many 'freed men' (*liberti*) played an important part in the counsels of the state; but when a state was organized on a foundation of slavery the problems of education were obviously different from those which face us at the present time when all labour is free. Ancient educationalists, practical and theoretical, did not take the slave-class into consideration.

They regarded education as a method of training which would fit the free citizen to take his proper place in the State, primarily for the State's, not the individual's, advantage; they did not aim at training him to earn his living either in a trade or a profession, except that public life at Rome, though hardly in the Greek states, was a lucrative profession. Thus ancient education may be said in general to have had an aristocratic bias, since it was designed chiefly and primarily for the upper classes of the community. In the humanistic education of the Renaissance and subsequent ages the same bias is discernible, for though the lower classes are not excluded, we are concerned mostly with the proper education of a gentleman.

At the present day in all civilized states the net of education is wider. The underlying principle is social efficiency, and the various systems are based on the belief that education is good for all classes; that, quite apart from technical skill, the stimulus to the intelligence which education provides will in the long run result in better work by the individual and will therefore be to the advantage of the community. There is, further, this advantage in universal education, that it gives an opening for individual merit, and those who have done well in the elementary stage have every opportunity for proceeding to a higher stage and thus rising above the level on which they were born.

3

WE HAVE SEEN that, while the Greeks were content to study their own literature, and knew nothing of any other, the Roman boy, as soon as Greek methods were introduced into Rome, was instructed normally in two languages, Greek and Latin, with a tendency sometimes to neglect his native tongue. In precisely the same way children of the age of the Renaissance were taught Latin at the expense of Italian or whatever was the language of their country. It has been mentioned that Dante was ridiculed by some of his contemporaries for writing in Italian.[6] In a similar fashion the English public schools, down to a time within living memory, taught their boys a great deal of the languages and the literatures of Greece and Rome, but almost entirely neglected the magnificent heritage of their native literature. Thus, at the end of the eighteenth century, the ordinary curriculum of English public schools consisted entirely of Greek and Latin; other subjects, such as writing, dancing, French, and drawing, were regarded as reputable accomplishments, and could be studied at Rugby on half holidays.[7] This was before the institution of organized games, so that it was perhaps thought necessary to find some not too serious occupation for the boys in their spare time. Similarly at Eton, for two hours on holidays and one hour on half holidays boys went into school to learn writing, arithmetic, ancient geography, elementary algebra, and occasionally Euclid. It was not till 1851 that mathematics obtained a place among the regular school-subjects.[8] Boys were, however, expected and to some extent encouraged to read English literature, and Greek and Roman history, in their leisure hours, and doubtless a small minority took advantage of such opportunities; but by far the greater number confined their energies to such studies as were compulsory. Yet even at this time the more enlightened educators had some searchings of heart, and we find James, headmaster of Rugby (1800), writing to the newly appointed headmaster of Shrewsbury and urging him to give the boys at least one lesson in English every week.[9] Development was even hampered by authority, as, for instance, when in 1805 it was ruled in the Court of Chancery that 'Grammar' signified the classical languages, and therefore endowed Grammar Schools were not justified in devoting part of their income to the teaching of modern languages and subjects of commercial utility.

Against the long dominion of the Classics there came an inevitable reaction when scientific education began to assert its claims, and for a time the air was filled with the clamours of those who asserted that the classical education was an anachronism, and that the only rational and useful form of education was one on scientific lines. The result was the institution in English schools of Modern Sides, wherein Mathematics, the Natural Sciences, and, in some cases, modern languages, took the place of the Classics as the standard school-subjects. This was good in its way, but the initial mistake in this movement was to let the pendulum swing too far. The scientists were divorced from Letters as thoroughly as the classical boys were excluded from the study of Science. This has been carried to extremes in England by the policy of certain schools which, with a view to gaining scholarships at the Universities, encourage their promising pupils to specialize at the age of fourteen, or thereabouts, in some narrow scientific field, not realizing, or not caring to realize, that an individual who spends his life, so to speak, in making the heads of pins, though he become an expert in the minutiae of the specialized trade, will in the end know little or nothing of metal-working in general; and the maxims of Industry do not apply to Life as a whole. The results of this intensive study are in many cases deplorable, and it is more than doubtful whether a scientist so trained can, even in his own sphere, be as useful as one whose education has a broader basis. Thus Science, though it could make out a strong case for reform, went too far, and we have begun to realize that over-specialization in scientific study can be as noxious as any other kind of specialization. The true solution lies in a compromise. *Trivium* and *Quadrivium* — literary and scientific studies — should both have their place; thus we keep to the spirit of the mediaeval system, though we change the content of the courses; but education should be as broad as possible, and should not be condemned because it does not seem, *prima facie,* to equip the youth for any specialized business or vocation. In the long run, those who have received a liberal education will in most cases outstrip those who lack it. We are coming round again to the Greek view that the best preparation for citizenship lies not in any specialized training, but in an all-round development of the mental faculties.

NOTES AND REFERENCES
BIBLIOGRAPHY

NOTES AND REFERENCES

INTRODUCTION

1. *Republic,* 7. 525 *sqq.;* 4. 419–20.
2. *ibid.,* 3. 395–400.
3. *ibid.,* 10. 605–607; 3. 395–6.
4. Horace, *Epistles,* II. 2. 43; G. Boissier, *Cicero and his Friends;* Cicero, *Brutus,* 91. 316; Nepos, *Life of Atticus,* 2, etc.

CHAPTER I

1. The boys in Crete were fed at the public expense, in contrast to the Spartan custom.
2. The chief authorities for Lycurgus are Xenophon's *Lacedaemonian Constitution;* Aristotle's *Politics,* II. 10 2; II. 12. 1–2; etc. Plutarch's *Life of Lycurgus.* The chronology of his life is hopelessly confused; see Grote, *History of Greece,* Part II, Chapter 6. The historian Ephorus, quoted by Strabo, X. 482, asserts that Lycurgus met Homer at Chios; another tradition, recorded by Aristotle, *Pol.,* II. 12. 7, made him a pupil of Thales.
3. Xenophon, *Lac. Const.,* Ch. 2.
4. Isocrates, *Panathenaicus,* §§ 209, 251; Plato, *Hippias Major,* 285 C.
5. Plut., *Lyc.,* 18; Cicero, *Tusc. Disp.,* V. 27. 77.
6. Xen., *Lac. Const.,* Ch. 4.
7. Gylippus and Lysander were notable exceptions.
8. Plut., *Lyc.,* 28. Plato, though he would not have countenanced such barbarity, approved of the general principle of a secret police force, and provided for it in the constitution outlined in his latest work, the *Laws* (pp. 633 C and 763 B).
9. *Pol.,* II. 4. 4.

CHAPTER II

1. Aesch., *contra Timarch.*, § 9.
2. Herod., VI. 27.
3. Plutarch, *Them.*, 10.
4. Mahaffy, *Ancient Greek Education*, p. 54.
5. Thuc., VII. 29.
6. T. Hudson Williams, *An education bill from ancient Greece*, Cambridge, 1917.
7. *ibid.*, and Whibley, *Companion to Greek Studies*, § 637.
8. Plut., *Alcib.*, 7.
9. *de Corona*, § 258.
10. Meineke, *Com. Frag.*, IV. 698.
11. Demos., *c. Con.*, §§ 3–5.
12. *Pol.*, VIII. 2. 4.
13. *Econ.*, IV. 3.
14. *Laws*, 846 D.
15. Plato, *Clitophon*, 409 B; *Rep.*, 421 E.
16. Xen., *Econ.*, VII. 5.
17. Herod., VIII. 75.
18. Eur., *Med.*, 1001–1018, etc.
19. *supra*, p. 26.
20. Thuc., VII. 29; Plato, *Laws*, 808; Lucian, *Parasite*, 61; *Amores*, 44–5.
21. Theophr., *Characters*, 30.
22. Plato, *Prot.*, 326, Demos., *de Cor.*, 258.
23. Athen., X. 453.
24. Dion. Hal., *de admir. vi dic.*, 52.
25. Aristophanes, *Wasps*, 656; Polyb., V. 26; cf. Becker, *Charikles*, p. 233.
26. Xen., *Symp.*, III. 5.
27. *Erastae*, p. 132.
28. *Theaet.*, p. 147 D.
29. Plato, *Prot.*, 325–6.
30. *Pol.*, VIII. 3. 7.
31. *Clouds*, 961–1023.
32. Aristotle, *Pol.*, VIII. 5. 7.; Plato, *Prot.*, 325–6.
33. Except in dramatic and religious performances.

34. *Pol.*, VIII. 3. 2.
35. *Pol.*, VIII. 3. 7; VIII. 6. 2.
36. Plato, *Prot.*, 325–6.
37. *Theaet.*, 144.
38. *supra*, p. 40.
39. *Cyrop.*, I. 4. 4.
40. *Symp.*, III. 13.
41. *Amores*, 44.
42. Thuc., I. 105.
43. *Ath. Pol.*, Ch. 42; *Corp. Inscr. Att.*, vol. iv.
44. Plut., *de educ. puer.*, 7; Diog. Laert., II. 72.
45. Plut., *Lives of the X Orators*, 4.
46. Diog. Laert., VII. 163, and Athen., IV. 168.
47. Plato, *Prot.*, 310, 315.
48. *Clouds*, *passim*.
49. It is to be noted that we owe to the philosophical schools the first organized study of various sciences. Aristotle, famous for his *Ethics* and *Metaphysics*, was equally distinguished for his writings on general Natural History, Physics, Biology, etc. His successor, Theophrastus, was the first great botanist. Plato himself was an able mathematician, though not by any means the founder of the science. His successors carried on the tradition. Cf. Sir T. L. Heath, *A Survey of Greek Mathematics*, p. 171, Camb. Univ. Press, 1930.
50. Pliny, on the authority of Varro, relates how the Ptolemies, jealous of the growth of the library of Pergamum in the century, prohibited the export of papyrus for the making of books. Consequently the Pergamenes were forced to use other materials, and invented or improved the manufacture of parchment which was called, from its place of origin, 'pergamene,' of which the modern name is a corruption. The story, if not literally true, is typical of the attitude of Alexandria. See Pliny, *Nat. Hist.*, XIII. 11. 21. 70.

CHAPTER III

1. See in general *Republic*, Bks. 4 and 5; *Laws*, Bk. 7. Preliminary education, *Rep.*, 2. 376; 4. 429–30; 7. 521–2.

2. Education, more widely understood, begins, however, at an even earlier stage, in the games of childhood: *Rep.*, 4. 425 A; 7. 536; *Laws,* I. 643.

3. *Rep.*, 7. 537 *sqq.*

4. *Rep.*, 5. 460.

5. *Rep.*, 5. 467; 7. 537.

6. *Rep.*, 5. 451–3; 456. *Laws,* 7. 805.

7. Xenophanes, *frag.* 7.

8. Pindar, *Olymp.*, 1. 82.

9. Plato, *Ion,* p. 541.

10. *Rep.*, 2. 377 *sqq.*; 3. 388, 408.

11. *Rep.*, 2. 377; 3. 391.

12. *Rep.*, 3. 401, B–C.

13. *Cyrop.*, I. Ch. 2.

14. Plato, *Rep.*, 2. 368 and books 8 and 9 *passim;* Aristotle, *Nic. Eth.*, I. 1094b.

15. *Pol.*, VIII. 2. 1. Aristotle, like Plato, is here considering the proper education for an ideal State, but whereas Plato's *Republic* is an oligarchy, the government for which Aristotle is providing is of a more popular nature. Aristotle considered Monarchy, under ideal conditions, to be the best, but thought it as a rule impracticable.

16. *Pol.*, II. Chs. 1–5.

17. *Eth. Nic.*, X. 7. 1177b. 20.

18. *Pol.*, VIII. 2. 4–5.

19. *Pol.*, VIII. 6. 7.

20. *Nic. Eth.*, I. 1103a. 20.

21. *ibid.*

22. *Pol.*, Bk. VII. 14. 13.

23. Isoc., *Antid.*, § 180.

24. *ibid.*, 184 *sqq.*

25. *προκοπὴ εἰς ἀρετήν.*

26. *op. cit.*, p. 456.

27. *supra,* p. 64; cf. Plut., *quomodo adolescens poetas audire debeat.*

28. *de vita et poesi Homeri,* II. 74; 92; 161.

29. *ibid.*, 212.

30. cf. *The Lives, passim.*

31. *de Musica,* pp. 1136–1142.

32. *de recta ratione audiendi,* 48.
33. *Sympos.,* II. 5; and *Inst. Lacon.*
34. *de sanitate tuenda.*
35. cf. also the treatises *de esu carnium.*

CHAPTER IV

1. *Odes,* III. 6. 37.
2. IV. 3.
3. Plautus (254–184 B.C.) is the earliest writer to mention a school, using the term *ludus litterarius* (*Merc.,* 2. 2. 32). Tacitus (*Dial.,* 28 *sqq.*) speaks of early home training under the care of the mother or some other female relative. Varro (ap. Non., 77. 3) mentions that in early days boys used to sing *carmina antiqua* at banquets. Pliny (*Epp.,* VIII. 14. 4–6) writes thus of education in early times: 'Each had his own father as instructor, and to those who had no father, the oldest and most distinguished citizen stood in the father's place.' Cf. Plautus, *Most.,* 126–7.
4. Pliny, *Epp.,* VIII. 14; Aulus Gellius, I. 23. 4.
5. Cicero, *de Amic.,* § 1. Ego autem a patre ita eram deductus ad Scaevolam sumpta virili toga ut, quoad possem et liceret, a senis latere nunquam discederem. Cf. Tacitus, *Dial.,* 34.
6. Cic., *de Leg.,* II. 4. 9 and 23. 59.
7. According to the opinion of the best authorities the figure of the she-wolf is certainly original; the twins are, as certainly, an example of Renaissance work. Mr. Last places the wolf as early as 500 B.C. (*Cambridge Ancient History,* vol. VII. p. 366.)
8. Plut., *Roman Questions,* 59.
9. Plut., *Rom.,* 6.
10. Livy, III. 44. 6. Livy also mentions schools at Falerii (V. 27) and at Tusculum in the time of Camillus (VI. 25).
11. Suetonius, *de Gram.,* 1.
12. i.e., by the study of subjects through which, as

Cicero puts it: puerorum mentes ad humanitatem fingerentur atque virtutem. Cicero, *de Or.*, III. 58.

13. Plut., *Cato,* 20.

14. We might apply to him also the famous line of Lucan: Victrix causa deis placuit, sed victa Catoni.

15. Cicero, *de Senect.*, §§ 3 and 38; Plutarch, *Cato,* 2.

16. Wordsworth, *Fragments and Specimens of Early Latin,* p. 342.

17. *Epist. ad Marcum filium,* Wordsworth, p. 342.

18. Pliny, *Nat. Hist.*, XXIX. 1. 8. 15. Wordsworth, p. 337 (*fr.* 160).

19. *Rhet. Lat. Minores,* ed. Halm, p. 374.

20. Plut., *Aemilius,* 6, etc.

21. Polybius, XXXII. 9; Plausanias, VII. 10.

22. *Sat.*, III. 244–301.

23. *Sat.*, I. 6. 72 *sqq.*

24. Juvenal, VII, 225, refers to the smoke of lanterns in the school-room: other references are Ovid, *Am.*, I. 13. 17; Martial, IX. 68. 3 and XII. 75. 5.

25. Martial, XIV. 223. Surgite, iam vendit pueris ientacula pistor.

26. Suet., *Aug.*, 94 and *Gram.*, 18; Juv., XI. 137.

27. e.g. Horace and Virgil, in Juv., VII. 226.

28. The *tabula Iliaca* is figured in *Corpus Inscr. Graec.*, vol. iii, p. 845 (No. 6125). It consists of a gypsum tablet covered with incised line-drawings and inscriptions, and was found in the ruins of a temple at Bovillae, where we know that there was a *sacellum* of the Julian family (Tac., *Ann.*, II. 41). It has been suggested, but this is mere conjecture, that the tablet was used in the education of the young Octavius (Augustus). Other pictures of this type are contained in the same volume of Inscriptions — e.g. No. 5984 (Labours of Heracles) and 6020 (Battle of Arbela).

29. Propertius, IV. 3. 37: Cogor et a tabula pictos ediscere mundos.

30. 'Crustula,' Hor., *Sat.*, I. 1. 25.

31. Quint., I. 1. 26.

32. V. 14. 31.

33. Hor., *Epist.*, II. 1. 70; Suet., *de Gram.*, 9; Cicero, *pro. Rosc. Com.* § 31; Seneca, *Epist.*, 94. 9.

34. Martial, IX. 68.

35. Quint., I. 3. 14.

36. Macrobius, *Sat.*, I. 10; Pliny, *Epist.*, VIII. 7; Hor., *Epist.*, II. 1. 197; Mart., V. 84.

37. Varro, ap. Non., 214. Expectant nundinas, ut magister dimittat lusum.

38. Hor., *Sat.*, I. 6. 75: Ibant octonis referentes Idibus aera; Martial, X. 62: aestate pueri si valent, satis discunt. But this may also be interpreted to mean that during the hot weather you must not be severe nor expect too much from the boys.

39. Macrob., *Sat.*, I. 12. 7; cf. Ovid, *Fasti,* III. 829 *sqq.* (the Quinquatrus as the beginning of the school-year).

40. *Epist.*, II. 2. 42; II. 1. 69.

41. Suet., *Gram.*, 16; Hor., *Epist.*, I. 20. 17.

42. Thuc., I. 138.

43. e.g., Cicero and Quintilian.

44. Quint., I. VIII. 5.

45. Suet., *Gram.*, 16; Tac., *Dial.*, 12.

46. Cic., *Ep.*, VI. 18. 5; Ovid, *Tristia,* II. 70; Statius, *Silvae,* II. 1. 114; Ausonius, *Protr. ad Nep.*, 46; Augustine, *de Civ. Dei,* II. 8.

47. Quint., I. 9. 1; 6.

48. Quint., I. 4, 2–5.

49. Suet., *Tib.*, 70.

50. Quint., I. 4. 4.

51. Cicero, *de nat. deor.*, II. 41. 104.; *ad Att.* II. 1.; Quint., X. 5.; Mackail's *Latin Literature;* Pliny, *Epist.*, VII. 4. 2.

52. Wilkins, *Rom. Educ.*, p. 74.

53. *supra,* p. 115, and Quint., II. 1. 3.

54. Quint., II. 4. 2; 15; 18–20, etc. It is interesting to note that this kind of composition is actually based on the practice not of a rhetorician but a philosopher. Plato's *Republic,* which, by means of various arguments and digressions, supports throughout ten books the theme that

'Justice is better than Injustice,' might be regarded as the prototype of such essays.

55. Cicero, *Brut.*, 90; 310, says that he himself declaimed both in Greek and Latin; cf. Suet., *de rhet*, 1. For 'commonplaces' see Juvenal, I. 16; Nettleship, *Essays*, ii. p. 112.

56. *Sat.*, I. 15–16.

57. Horace, *Odes*, III. 6.

CHAPTER V

1. Quintilian actually uses Cato's phrase (XII. 1. 1). Cicero's requirement is a *doctus orator*, a cultured speaker (*de Or.*, III. 143); but he implies that goodness is necessary (*de Or.*, II. 85). To Quintilian a bad man cannot be a good orator.

2. *de Or.*, II. 1, and II. 72.

3. *ad Q. fr.*, III. 3. 1–4, etc.

4. *de Or.*, III. 127.

5. Varro named nine, Vitruvius eleven [lit., drawing, geometry, optics, arith., hist., philos., music, med., law, astr.], Seneca only five. These were called ἐγκύκλιοι in Greek (Sen., *Epp.*, 88. 20).

6. *de Or.*, I. 187.

7. *ad. Att.*, IV. 15. 10; *ad Q. fr.*, II. 4. 2.

8. *de Off.*, I. 1.

9. *de Or.*, I. 20; and I. 72–3.

10. *de Or.*, I. 48.

11. *de Or.*, II. 62–64.

12. Vitruvius, *de Arch.*, I. 1. 3.

13. Quint., I. 1. 1–8.

14. I. 1. 15–20.

15. I. 1. 24 *sqq.*; 36.

16. I. 1. 12–13.

17. I. 2. 1–5; I. 2. 28.

18. I. 3. 13–14.

19. I. 3. 8–11.

20. Quint., *Prooem.*, § 1.

CHAPTER VI

1. Martial, I. 61 7–12, gives a remarkable list of Spaniards distinguished in rhetoric and literature in the first century A.D. Rutilius Namatianus, *de reditu suo,* I. 66: Urbem fecisti quod prius orbis erat.

2. Tacitus, *Ann.,* III. 43. The school of Autun was restored by Constantius Chlorus 297, A.D. cf. Eumen., *pro rest. schol.,* 14.

3. Tac., *Agr.,* 21.

4. Juv., 15. 110–112.

   Nunc totus Graias nostrasque habet orbis Athenas,
   Gallia causidicos docuit facunda Britannos,
   De conducendo loquitur iam rhetore Thule.

5. Ausonius, *Professores,* IV. 7–9.

6. Strabo, IV. 1. 5.

7. Sueton., *de illust. gramm.,* ch's. 3 and 11.

8. cf. *infra* p. 170.

9. Sueton, *Claudius,* 42; *Nero,* 49.

10. Sueton., *Vespasian,* 18.

11. Nerva recalled from exile the rhetorician Dio Chrysostom; Trajan conferred on the sophist Polemo the right of free travel by land and sea. (Philost., 532.)

12. Philost., 549; Pausanias, I. 18. 9; Dio, 69. 16.

13. Aurelius Victor, *Epit.,* 14; *Dig.,* 1. 4, etc. Julius Capitolinus, *Antoninus Pius,* 11 (in *Historia Augusta*).

14. See Walden, *Universities of Ancient Greece,* p. 87, n. 2, for a discussion of the evidence.

15. Philost., 566; Dio Cassius, LXXII. 31.

16. Eumen., *pro inst. schol.,* 14.

17. *Cod. Theod.,* XIII. 3. 1–3, and *Cod. Just.,* X. 52.

18. *Cod. Theod.,* XIII. 3. 5.

19. *Eunap.,* 493.

20. *Cod. Theod.,* XIII. 3. 11.

21. *ibid.,* XIII. 3. 6.

22. Lamprid., *Alexander Severus,* 44.

23. Philost., 583.

24. Philost., 582.

25. Philost., 612, 620; cf. Pliny, *Ep.*, II. 3, on the rhetor Isaeus.

26. Lib., I. 16. 1; Eunap., p. 75, etc. For 'Nations,' cf. Philost., 571, 613; Greg. Naz., *Or.*, 43. 17.

27. Greg. Naz., *Or.*, 43. 15, 16.

28. Eunap., 483.

29. Lib., I. 60.

30. Philost., 483–4.

CHAPTER VII

1. Notably St. Augustine.

2. See R. L. Poole, *History of Med. Thought,* p. 8.

3. See J. W. Adamson, *Short History of Education,* p. 12.

4. Adamson, *op. cit.,* p. 1.

5. See Woodward, *Vittorino da Feltre and Other Humanist Educators,* p. 141.

6. *de ingenuis moribus* (1404 A.D.)

7. Woodward, p. 184.

8. For all details of Vittorino's life and teaching I am indebted to Woodward, *op. cit.*

9. *vide* the dialogue of Lionardo of Arezzo, pp. 60–65 (Woodward 41–2).

10. Woodward, pp. 39, 40, 49, 50.

11. cf. Guarino, *de ordine docendi et studendi,* trans. by Woodward, p. 165.

12. See *Value of the Classics* by A. F. West, *infra* p. 182.

13. Guarino, p. 162 (Woodward).

14. P. S. Allen, *Opus Epist. Erasmi,* vol. iii, pp. 542–546.

15. Allen, *op. cit.,* vol. iii, p. 37.

16. *ibid.,* vol. i, p. 508.

17. *vide* J. H. Lupton, *Life of John Colet, Dean of St. Paul's,* p. 279. "I charge the masters that they teach always what is the best, and instruct the children in Greek and Latin in reading to them such authors that hath with wisdom joined the pure chaste eloquence." (Spelling modernized.)

CHAPTER VIII

1. *Value of the Classics,* edited by A. F. West, Princeton University Press, 1917.

2. Montaigne, *Essays,* 20, *Of the Education of Children:* "We did Latin at such a rate, that it overflowed to the neighbouring villages, where there yet remain, that have established themselves by custom, several Latin appellations of artizans and their tools." (Charles Cotton's translation, 1700.) At the present day, in the University town of Leiden, there may be seen on lodging-houses the notice *Cubicula locanda.*

3. *The Scholemaster,* Bk. 1. p. 28.: 'Loquendo, male loqui discunt.' (Quoted from Cicero.) Budaeus, quoted by Ascham (*ibid.*), complained that the practice of speaking Latin, at table and elsewhere, had completely ruined his style.

4. Adamson, p. 227.

5. Among the books used by the father of the present writer at Marlborough College in 1855 were The Delphin *Virgil,* with Latin notes and paraphrase; a Homer with scholia in Greek; and Schrevelius' Lexicon (Greek into Latin). Classical texts with English notes were not, however, entirely unknown.

6. *supra,* p. 172.

7. Adamson, p. 224.

8. *ibid.,* p. 226.

9. *ibid.,* p. 225.

SELECT BIBLIOGRAPHY OF THE CHIEF AUTHORITIES CONSULTED

A. ANCIENT AUTHORS

WITH a few exceptions the original texts of the classical writers are accessible in the *Oxford Series of Classical Texts* or in B. G. Teubner's *Bibliotheca Classica* (Leipzig). Many have been published, or are in process of publication, in the *Loeb Classical Library,* each volume containing text, translation, and notes. In addition to these, certain other editions and translations are here noted, in brackets, after the authors' names.

ARISTOTLE, 384–322 B.C. (*Politics,* tr. B. Jowett, ed. by H. W. C. Davis; *Ethics,* tr. J. E. C. Welldon).

CICERO, 106–43 B.C. (*de Oratore,* ed. A. S. Wilkins).

EUNAPIUS, b. 347 A.D.

GREGORY OF NAZIANZUS, 329–390 A.D. (in Migne's *Patrologia Graeca,* vols. 35–8).

ISOCRATES, 436–338 B.C.

LIBANIUS, 314–392(?) A.D.

LUCIAN, ca. 120–ca. 190 A.D.

PHILOSTRATUS, ca. 182–245 A.D.

PLATO, 427(?)–347 B.C., esp. *Republic* and *Laws* (tr. B. Jowett).

PLUTARCH, first century A.D., *Lives* (numerous translations), *Moralia.*

QUINTILIAN, ca. 35–118(?) A.D.

SENECA THE ELDER, born ca. 55 B.C. (*The Suasoriae,* ed. W. A. Edward, 1928).

SUETONIUS, born ca. 75 A.D.

XENOPHON, ca. 430–ca. 354 B.C. (tr. H. G. Dakyns).

BIBLIOGRAPHY

B. MODERN AUTHORITIES

ADAMSON, J. W., *A Short History of Education.* Cambridge, England, 1919.

ALLEN, P. S., *Opus epistolarum Erasmi.* Oxford, 1906–1928.

BECKER, W. A., *Charicles:* illustrations of the private life of the Greeks (English edition). London, 1845.

——, *Gallus:* Roman Scenes of the time of Augustus (Eng. ed.). London, 1866.

BIGG, CHARLES, *The Church's task under the Roman Empire.* Oxford, 1905.

The Cambridge Ancient History (vols. i–viii published to date).

DREYER, JAMES, *Greek Education.* Cambridge, England, 1912.

FREEMAN, K. J., *Schools of Hellas.* London, 1907.

GWYNN, AUBREY; S. J., *Roman Education from Cicero to Quintilian.* Oxford, 1926.

HAARHOFF, T., *Schools of Gaul.* Oxford, 1920.

POOLE, R. L., *Illustrations of the History of Mediaeval Thought.* London, 1884.

RASHDALL, H., *Universities of Europe in the Middle Ages.* Oxford, 1895.

SANDYS, SIR J. E., *A Companion to Latin Studies.*[2] Cambridge, England, 1913.

WALDEN, J. W. H., *The Universities of Ancient Greece.* New York and London, 1912.

WESTAWAY, KATE M., *The Educational Theory of Plutarch.* London, 1922.

WHIBLEY, L., *A Companion to Greek Studies.* Cambridge, England, 1931.

WILKINS, A. S., *Roman Education.* Cambridge, England, 1905.

WOODWARD, W. H., *Vittorino da Feltre and other Humanist Educators.* Cambridge, England, 1912.

BIBLIOGRAPHY

I. [illegible]

ADAMSON, J. W., *A Short History of Education.* Cambridge, England, [illegible]

[illegible], F., *Die attische Beredsamkeit.* Leipzig, 1868-1880.

BECKER, W. A., *Charicles, Illustrations of the Private Life of the Ancient Greeks.* London, 1866.

———, *Gallus, Roman Scenes of the Time of Augustus.* (Trans.) London, 1866.

BIGG, CHARLES, *The Church's Task under the Roman Empire.* Oxford, 1905.

The Cambridge Ancient History. Vols. I-VII published to date.

DREVER, JAMES, *Greek Education.* Cambridge, England, 1912.

FREEMAN, K. J., *Schools of Hellas.* London, 1907.

GWYNN, AUBREY, S. J., *Roman Education from Cicero to Quintilian.* Oxford, 1926.

[illegible]

POOLE, R. L., *Illustrations of the History of Medieval Thought.* London, 1884.

RASHDALL, H., *Universities of Europe in the Middle Ages.* Oxford, 1895.

SANDYS, SIR J. E., *A Companion to Latin Studies.* Cambridge, England, 1913.

WALDEN, J. W. H., *The Universities of Ancient Greece.* New York and London, 1912.

[illegible], KATE M., *The Educational Theory of Plutarch.* London, [illegible]

WHIBLEY, L., *A Companion to Greek Studies.* Cambridge, England, 1905.

WILKINS, A. S., *Roman Education.* Cambridge, England, [illegible]

WOODWARD, W. H., *Vittorino da Feltre and other Humanist Educators.* Cambridge, England, 1912.

CONTRIBUTORS TO THE
"OUR DEBT TO GREECE AND ROME FUND"
WHOSE GENEROSITY HAS MADE POSSIBLE THE LIBRARY

Our Debt to Greece and Rome

Philadelphia

Dr. Astley P. C. Ashhurst
Thomas G. Ashton
William L. Austin
John C. Bell
Henry H. Bonnell
Jasper Yeates Brinton
George Burnham, Jr.
John Cadwalader
Morris L. Clothier
Miss Clara Comegys
Miss Mary E. Converse
Arthur G. Dickson
William M. Elkins
H. H. Furness, Jr.
Thomas S. Gates
William P. Gest
John Gribbel
Miss M. S. Hinchman
Edward Hopkinson, Jr.
Samuel F. Houston
Charles Edward Ingersoll
John Story Jenks
Alba B. Johnson
Miss Nina Lea
Horatio G. Lloyd
George McFadden
Mrs. John Markoe
J. Willis Martin
Jules E. Mastbaum
J. Vaughan Merrick
David Milne
Effingham B. Morris
William R. Murphy
John S. Newbold
S. Davis Page (*memorial*)
Eli Kirk Price
Owen J. Roberts
Joseph G. Rosengarten
Miss Caroline Sinkler
William C. Sproul
John B. Stetson, Jr.
Dr. J. William White (*memorial*)
George D. Widener
Mrs. James D. Winsor
Owen Wister
The Philadelphia Society for the Promotion of Liberal Studies

Boston

Oric Bates (*memorial*)
Miss Mary H. Buckingham
Frederick P. Fish
William Amory Gardner
Joseph Clark Hoppin
William Caleb Loring
Miss Ellen F. Mason

Chicago

John C. Shaffer
Harold H. Swift
Herbert W. Wolff

Cincinnati

Herbert G. French
Charles Phelps Taft

Cleveland

Samuel Mather

Detroit

John W. Anderson
Dexter M. Ferry, Jr.
Henry G. Sherrard (*memorial*)

Doylestown, Pennsylvania

"A Lover of Greece and Rome"

Kansas City

Charles Baird

Lancaster

William H. Keller

New York

"Anonymous"
John Jay Chapman
Otto H. Kahn
Willard V. King
Thomas W. Lamont
Dwight W. Morrow
Mrs. D. W. Morrow
Senatori Societatis Philosophiae, ΦBK, gratias maximas agimus
Elihu Root
Mortimer L. Schiff
William Sloane
George W. Wickersham
Miss Nellie C. Williams
And one contributor, who has asked to have his name withheld:
Maecenas atavis edite regibus,
O et praesidium et dulce decus meum

Providence

John Nicholas Brown

Washington

The Greek Embassy at Washington, for the Greek Government

Our Debt to Greece and Rome

AUTHORS AND TITLES

AUTHORS AND TITLES

1. HOMER. *John A. Scott*, Northwestern University.
2. SAPPHO. *David M. Robinson*, The Johns Hopkins University.
3. EURIPIDES. *F. L. Lucas*, King's College, Cambridge.
4. ARISTOPHANES. *Louis E. Lord*, Oberlin College.
5. DEMOSTHENES. *Charles D. Adams*, Dartmouth College.
6. THE POETICS OF ARISTOTLE. *Lane Cooper*, Cornell University.
7. GREEK RHETORIC AND LITERARY CRITICISM. *W. Rhys Roberts*, Leeds University.
8. LUCIAN. *Francis G. Allinson*, Brown University.
9. CICERO AS PHILOSOPHER. *Nelson G. McCrea*, Columbia University.
10. CICERO AND HIS INFLUENCE. *John C. Rolfe*, University of Pennsylvania.
11. CATULLUS. *Karl P. Harrington*, Wesleyan University.
12. LUCRETIUS AND EPICUREANISM. *George Depue Hadzsits*, University of Pennsylvania.
13. OVID. *Edward Kennard Rand*, Harvard University.
14. HORACE. *Grant Showerman*, University of Wisconsin.
15. VIRGIL. *John William Mackail*, Balliol College, Oxford.
16. SENECA, THE PHILOSOPHER. *Richard Mott Gummere*, The William Penn Charter School.
17. APULEIUS. *Elizabeth Hazelton Haight*, Vassar College.
18. MARTIAL. *Paul Nixon*, Bowdoin College.
19. PLATONISM. *Alfred Edward Taylor*, University of Edinburgh.
20. ARISTOTELIANISM. *John L. Stocks*, University of Manchester.

AUTHORS AND TITLES

21. STOICISM. *Robert Mark Wenley*, University of Michigan.
22. LANGUAGE AND PHILOLOGY. *Roland G. Kent*, University of Pennsylvania.
23. AESCHYLUS AND SOPHOCLES. *J. T. Sheppard*, King's College, Cambridge.
24. GREEK RELIGION. *Walter Woodburn Hyde*, University of Pennsylvania.
25. ROMAN RELIGION. *Gordon J. Laing*, University of Chicago.
26. MYTHOLOGY. *Jane Ellen Harrison*, Newnham College, Cambridge.
27. ANCIENT BELIEFS IN THE IMMORTALITY OF THE SOUL. *Clifford H. Moore*, Harvard University.
28. STAGE ANTIQUITIES. *James Turney Allen*, University of California.
29. PLAUTUS AND TERENCE. *Gilbert Norwood*, University of Toronto.
30. ROMAN POLITICS. *Frank Frost Abbott*, Princeton University.
31. PSYCHOLOGY, ANCIENT AND MODERN. *G. S. Brett*, University of Toronto.
32. ANCIENT AND MODERN ROME. *Rodolfo Lanciani*, Rome.
33. WARFARE BY LAND AND SEA. *Eugene S. McCartney*, University of Michigan.
34. THE GREEK FATHERS. *James Marshall Campbell*, The Catholic University of America.
35. GREEK BIOLOGY AND MEDICINE. *Henry Osborn Taylor*, New York.
36. MATHEMATICS. *David Eugene Smith*, Teachers College, Columbia University.
37. LOVE OF NATURE AMONG THE GREEKS AND ROMANS. *H. R. Fairclough*, Leland Stanford Junior University.
38. ANCIENT WRITING. *B. L. Ullman*, University of Chicago.
39. THE FINE ARTS. *Arthur Fairbanks*, formerly of the Museum of Fine Arts, Boston.

40. ARCHITECTURE. *Alfred M. Brooks*, Swarthmore College.
41. ENGINEERING. *Alexander P. Gest*, Rensselaer Polytechnic Institute.
42. MODERN TRAITS IN OLD GREEK LIFE. *Charles Burton Gulick*, Harvard University.
43. ROMAN PRIVATE LIFE. *Walton Brooks McDaniel*, University of Pennsylvania.
44. GREEK AND ROMAN FOLKLORE. *William Reginald Halliday*, University of Liverpool.
45. ANCIENT EDUCATION. *J. F. Dobson*, University of Bristol.

GREEK POLITICS.
GREEK HISTORIANS.
ROMAN HISTORIANS. *Guglielmo Ferrero*, Florence.
ROMAN LAW. *Roscoe Pound*, Harvard Law School.
ROMAN POETRY AND ITS INFLUENCE UPON EUROPEAN CULTURE. *Paul Shorey*, University of Chicago.
ROMAN RHETORIC AND LITERARY CRITICISM.
CHRISTIAN LATIN WRITERS.
MUSIC.
ASTRONOMY AND ASTROLOGY.
ECONOMICS AND SOCIETY.

COLLEGE LIBRARY
ST.
JOSEPH'S
COLLEGE
1852
Phila., Pa.